SHAKESPEAREAN ORIGINALS:
FIRST EDITIONS

M. William Shak–speare:

HIS

*True Chronicle Historie of the life and
death of King LEAR and his three
Daughters.*

EDITED AND INTRODUCED BY
GRAHAM HOLDERNESS

PRENTICE HALL

HARVESTER WHEATSHEAF

First published 1995 by
Prentice Hall International (UK) Limited
Campus 400, Maylands Avenue
Hemel Hempstead
Hertfordshire HP2 7EZ
A division of
Simon & Schuster International Group

Designed by Geoff Green

Typeset in 11pt Bembo
by Photoprint, Torquay, Devon

Printed and bound in Great Britain by
Biddles Ltd, Guildford and King's Lynn

Library of Congress Cataloging-in-Publication Data

Shakespeare, William, 1564–1616.
    [King Lear]
    M. William Shak-speare, his true chronicle historie
of the life and death of King Lear and his three
daughters / edited and introduced by Graham Holderness.
        p.   cm. — (Shakespearean originals—First editions)
    Includes bibliographical references (p.).
    ISBN 0–13–355363–9
    1. Lear, King (Legendary character)—Drama.
2. Fathers and daughters—England—Drama.
I. Holderness, Graham.   II. Title.   III. Series.
PR2750.B19   1995
822.3'3—dc20   95–10120
                                                    CIP

British Library Cataloguing in Publication Data

A catalogue record for this book is available from
the British Library
ISBN 0–13–355363–9

1   2   3   4   5   99 98 97 96 95

10006065О1

Contents

General Introduction

T H I S series puts into circulation single annotated editions of early modern play-texts whose literary and theatrical histories have been overshadowed by editorial practices dominant since the eighteenth century.

The vast majority of Shakespeare's modern readership encounters his works initially through the standard modernised editions of the major publishing houses, whose texts form the basis of innumerable playhouse productions and classroom discussions. While these textualisations vary considerably in terms of approach and detail, the overwhelming impression they foster is not of diversity but uniformity: the same plays are reprinted in virtually identical words, within a ubiquitous, standardised format. Cumulatively, such texts serve to constitute and define a particular model of Shakespeare's work, conjuring up a body of writing which is given and stable, handed down by the author like holy writ. But the canonical status of these received texts is ultimately dependent not upon a divine creator, but upon those editorial mediations (rendered transparent by the discursive authority of the very texts they ostensibly serve) that shape the manner in which Shakespeare's works are produced and reproduced within contemporary culture.

Many modern readers of Shakespeare, lulled by long-established editorial traditions into an implicit confidence in the object of their attention, probably have little idea of what a sixteenth-century printed play-text actually looked like. Confronted with an example, she or he could be forgiven for recoiling before the intimidating display of linguistic and visual strangeness – antique type, non-standardised spelling, archaic orthographic conventions, unfamiliar and irregular speech prefixes, oddly placed stage directions, and

[1]

possibly an absence of Act and scene divisions. 'It looks more like Chaucer than Shakespeare,' observed one student presented with a facsimile of an Elizabethan text, neatly calling attention to the peculiar elisions through which Shakespeare is accepted as modern, while Chaucer is categorised as ancient. A student reading Chaucer in a modern translation knows that the text is a contemporary version, not a historical document. But the modern translations of Shakespeare which almost universally pass as accurate and authentic representations of an original – the standard editions – offer themselves as simultaneously historical document and accessible modern version – like a tidily restored ancient building.

The earliest versions of Shakespeare's works existed in plural and contested forms. Some nineteen of those plays modern scholars now attribute to Shakespeare (together with the non-dramatic verse) appeared in cheap Quarto format during his life, their theatrical provenance clearly marked by an emphasis upon the companies who owned and produced the plays rather than the author.[1] Where rival Quartos of a play were printed, these could contrast starkly: the Second Quarto of *The tragicall historie of Hamlet, prince of Denmarke* (1604), for example, is almost double the length of its First Quarto (1603) predecessor and renames many of the leading characters. In 1623, Shakespeare's colleagues Heminges and Condell brought out posthumously the prestigious and expensive First Folio, the earliest collected edition of his dramatic works. This included major works, such as *The Tragedy of Macbeth, Antonie and Cleopater*, and *The Tempest*, which had never before been published. It also contained versions of those plays, with the exception of *Pericles*, which had earlier appeared in Quarto versions which in some cases differ so markedly from their notional predecessors for them to be regarded not simply as variants of a single work, but as discrete textualisations independently framed within a complex and diversified project of cultural production; perhaps, even, in some senses, as separate plays. In the case of *Hamlet*, for example, the Folio includes some eighty lines which are not to be found in the Second Quarto, yet omits a fragment of around 230 lines which includes Hamlet's final soliloquy;[2] and far greater differences exist between certain other pairings.

This relatively fluid textual situation continued throughout the seventeenth century. Quartos of individual plays continued to appear sporadically, usually amended reprints of earlier editions, but occasionally introducing new works, such as the first publication of Shakespeare and Fletcher's *The two noble kinsmen* (1634), a play which was perhaps excluded from the Folio on the basis of its collaborative status.[3] The title of another work written in collaboration with Fletcher, *Cardenio*, was entered on the Stationer's Register of 1653, but it appears not to have been published and the play is now lost. The First Folio proved a commercial success and was reprinted in 1632, although again amended in detail. In 1663, a third edition appeared which in its 1664 reprinting assigned to Shakespeare seven plays, never before printed in folio, viz. *Pericles Prince of Tyre; The London prodigall; The history of Thomas Ld Cromwell; Sir John Oldcastle Lord Cobham; The Puritan widow; A Yorkshire tragedy; The tragedy of Locrine*. These attributions, moreover, were accepted uncritically by the 1685 Fourth Folio.

The assumptions underlying seventeenth-century editorial practice, particularly the emphasis that the latest edition corrects and subsumes all earlier editions, is rarely explicitly stated. It is graphically illustrated, though, by the Bodleian Library's decision to sell off as surplus to requirements the copy of the First Folio it had acquired in 1623 as soon as the enlarged 1663 edition came into its possession.[4] Eighteenth-century editors continued to work within this tradition. Rowe set his illustrated critical edition from the 1685 Fourth Folio, introducing further emendations and modernisations. Alexander Pope used Rowe as the basis of his own text, but he 'corrected' this liberally, partly on the basis of variants contained within the twenty-eight Quartos he catalogued but more often relying on his own intuitive judgement, maintaining that he was merely 'restoring' Shakespeare to an original purity which had been lost through 'arbitrary Additions, Expunctions, Transpositions of scenes and lines, Confusions of Characters and Persons, wrong application of Speeches, corruptions of innumerable passages'[5] introduced by actors. Although eighteenth-century editors disagreed fiercely over the principles of their task, all of them concurred in finding corruption at every point of textual transmission (and in Capell's case, composition), and sought the restoration of a perceived poetic genius: for Theobald, Warburton, Johnson and Steevens,

'The multiple sources of corruption justified editorial intervention; in principle at least, the edition that had received the most editorial attention, the most recent edition, was the purest because the most purified.'[6]

This conception of the editorial function was decisively challenged in theory and practice by Edmund Malone, who substituted the principles of archaeology for those of evolution. For Malone, there could be only one role for an editor: to determine what Shakespeare himself had written. Those texts which were closest to Shakespeare in time were therefore the only true authority; the accretions from editorial interference in the years which followed the publication of the First Folio and early Quartos had to be stripped away to recover the original. Authenticity, that is, was to be based on restoration understood not as improvement but as rediscovery. The methodology thus offered the possibility that the canon of Shakespeare's works could be established decisively, fixed for all time, by reference to objective, historical criteria. Henceforth, the text of Shakespeare was to be regarded, potentially, as monogenous, derived from a single source, rather than polygenous.

Malone's influence has proved decisive to the history of nineteenth- and twentieth-century bibliographic studies. Despite, however, the enormous growth in knowledge concerning the material processes of Elizabethan and Jacobean book production, the pursuit of Shakespeare's original words sanctioned a paradoxical distrust of precisely those early texts which Malone regarded as the touchstone of authenticity. Many assumed that these texts must themselves have been derived from some kind of authorial manuscript, and the possibility that Shakespeare's papers lay hidden somewhere exercised an insidious fascination upon the antiquarian imagination. Libraries were combed, lofts ransacked, and graves plundered, but the manuscripts have proved obstinately elusive, mute testimony to the low estimate an earlier culture had placed upon them once performance and publication had exhausted their commercial value.

Undeterred, scholars attempted to infer from the evidence of the early printed texts the nature of the manuscript which lay behind them. The fact that the various extant versions differed so considerably from each other posed a problem which could only be partially resolved by the designation of some as 'Bad Quartos', and therefore

General Introduction

non-Shakespearean; for even the remaining 'authorised' texts varied between themselves enormously, invariably in terms of detail and often in terms of substance. Recourse to the concept of manuscript authenticity could not resolve the difficulty, for such a manuscript simply does not exist.[7] Faced with apparent textual anarchy, editors sought solace in Platonic idealism: each variant was deemed an imperfect copy of a perfect (if unobtainable) paradigm. Once again, the editor's task was to restore a lost original purity, employing compositor study, collation, conflation and emendation.[8]

Compositor study attempts to identify the working practices of the individuals who set the early Quartos and the Folio, and thus differentiate the non-Shakespearean interference, stripping the 'veil of print from a text' and thus attempting 'to recover a number of precise details of the underlying manuscript'.[9] Collation, the critical comparison of different states of a text with a view to establishing the perfect condition of a particular copy, provided systematic classification of textual variations which could be regarded as putative corruptions. Emendation allows the editor to select one of the variations thrown up by collation and impose it upon the reading of the selected control text, or where no previous reading appeared satisfactory, to introduce a correction based upon editorial judgement. Conflation is employed to resolve the larger scale divergences between texts, so that, for example, the Folio *Tragedie of Hamlet, Prince of Denmarke* is often employed as the control text for modern editions of the play, but since it 'lacks' entire passages found only in the Second Quarto, these are often grafted on to the former to create the fullest 'authoritative' text.

The cuts to the Folio *Hamlet* may reflect, however, not a corruption introduced in the process of transmission, but a deliberate alteration to the text authorised by the dramatist himself. In recent years, the proposition that Shakespeare revised his work and that texts might therefore exist in a variety of forms has attracted considerable support. The most publicised debate has centred on the relationship of the Quarto *M. William Shak-speare: his true chronicle historie of the life and death of King Lear and his three daughters* and the Folio *Tragedie of King Lear*.[10] The editors of the recent Oxford Shakespeare have broken new ground by including both texts in their one-volume edition on the grounds that the *Tragedie* represents an authorial revision of the earlier *Historie*, which is sufficiently radical to justify classifying it as a separate play. Wells and Taylor founded their revisionist position upon a recognition of the fact that Shakespeare was primarily a working *dramatist* rather than literary author and that he addressed his play-texts towards a particular audience of theatrical professionals who were expected to flesh out the bare skeleton of the performance script: 'The written text of any such manuscript thus depended upon an unwritten para-text which always accompanied it: an invisible life-support system of stage directions, which Shakespeare could expect his first audience to supply, or which those first readers would expect Shakespeare himself to supply orally.'[11] They are thus more open than many of their predecessors to the possibility that texts reflect their theatrical provenance and therefore that a plurality of authorised texts may exist, at least for certain of the plays.[12] They remain, however, firmly author centred – the invisible life-support system can ultimately always be traced back to the dramatist himself and the plays remain under his parental authority.[13]

What, however, if it were not Shakespeare but the actor Burbage who suggested, or perhaps insisted on, the cuts to *Hamlet*? Would the Folio version of the play become unShakespearean? How would we react if we *knew* that the Clown spoke 'More than is set down' and that his ad libs were recorded? Or that the King's Men sanctioned additions by another dramatist for a Court performance? Or that a particular text recorded not the literary script of a play but its performance script? Of course, in one sense we cannot know these things. But drama, by its very nature, is overdetermined, the product of multiple influences simultaneously operating across a single site of cultural production. Eyewitness accounts of performances of the period suggest something of the provisionality of the scripts Shakespeare provided to his theatrical colleagues:

> After dinner on the 21st of september, at about two o'clock, I went with my companions over the water, and in the thatched playhouse saw the tragedy of the first Emperor Julius with at least fifteen characters very well acted. At the end of the comedy they danced according to their custom with extreme elegance. Two in men's clothes and two in women's gave this performance, in wonderful combination with each other.[14]

[6]

This passage offers what can seem a bizarre range of codes; the thatched playhouse, well-acted tragedy, comic aftermath and elegant transvestite dance, hardly correspond to the typology of Shakespearean drama our own culture has appropriated. The Swiss tourist Thomas Platter was in fact fortunate to catch the curious custom of the jig between Caesar and the boy dressed as Caesar's wife, for by 1612 'all Jigs, Rhymes and Dances' after plays had been 'utterly abolished' to prevent 'tumults and outrages whereby His Majesty's Peace is often broke'.[15] Shakespeare, however, is the 'author' of the spectacle Platter witnessed only in an extremely limited sense; in this context the dramatist's surname functions not simply to authenticate a literary masterpiece, but serves as a convenient if misleading shorthand term alluding to the complex material practices of the Elizabethan and Jacobean theatre industry.[16] It is in the latter sense that the term is used in this series.

Modern theoretical perspectives have destabilised the notion of the author as transcendent subject operating outside history and culture. This concept is in any event peculiarly inappropriate when applied to popular drama of the period. It is quite possible that, as Terence Hawkes argues, 'The notion of a single "authoritative" text, immediately expressive of the plenitude of its author's mind and meaning, would have been unfamiliar to Shakespeare, involved as he was in the collaborative enterprise of dramatic production and notoriously unconcerned to preserve in stable form the texts of most of his plays.'[17] The script is, of course, an integral element of drama, but it is by no means the only one. This is obvious in forms of representation, such as film, dependent on technologies which emphasise the role of the *auteur* at the expense of that of the writer. But even in the early modern theatre, dramatic realisation depended not just upon the scriptwriter,[18] but upon actors, entrepreneurs, promptbook keepers, audiences, patrons, etc.; in fact, the entire wide range of professional and institutional interests constituting the theatre industry of the period.

Just as the scriptwriter cannot be privileged over all other influences, nor can any single script. It is becoming clear that within Elizabethan and Jacobean culture, around each 'Shakespeare' play there circulated a wide variety of texts, performing different theatrical functions and adopting different shapes in different contexts of production. Any of these contexts may be of interest to the modern reader. The so-called Bad Quartos, for example, are generally marginalised as piratically published versions based upon the memorial reconstructions of the plays by bit-part actors. But even if the theory of memorial reconstruction is correct (and it is considerably more controversial than is generally recognised[19]), these quarto texts would provide a unique window on to the plays as they were originally performed and open up exciting opportunities for contemporary performance.[20] They form part, that is, of a rich diversity of textual variation which is shrouded by those traditional editorial practices which have sought to impose a single, 'ideal' paradigm.

In this series we have sought to build upon the pioneering work of Wells and Taylor, albeit along quite different lines. They argue, for example, that

> The lost manuscripts of Shakespeare's work are not the fiction of an idealist critic, but particular material objects which happen at a particular time to have existed, and at another particular time to have been lost, or to have ceased to exist. Emendation does not seek to construct an ideal text, but rather to restore certain features of a lost material object (that manuscript) by correcting certain apparent deficiencies in a second material object (this printed text) which purports to be a copy of the first. Most readers will find this procedure reasonable enough.[21]

The important emphasis here is on the relative status of the two forms, manuscript and printed text: the object of which we can have direct knowledge, the printed text, is judged to be corrupt by conjectural reference to the object of which we can by definition have no direct knowledge, the uncorrupted (but non-existent) manuscript. This corresponds to no philosophical materialism we have encountered. The editors of *Shakespearean Originals* reject the claim that it is possible to construct a rehabilitated text reflecting a form approximating Shakespeare's artistic vision.[22] Instead we prefer to embrace the early printed texts as authentic material objects, the concrete forms from which all subsequent editions ultimately derive.

We therefore present within this series particular textualisations of plays which are not necessarily canonical or indeed even written by *William Shakespeare, Gent,* in the traditional sense; but which nevertheless represent important facets of Shakespearean drama. In the same way that we have rejected the underlying principles of traditional editorial practice, we have also approached traditional editorial procedures with extreme caution, preferring to let the texts speak for themselves with a minimum of editorial mediation. We refuse to allow speculative judgements concerning the exact contribution of the various individuals involved in the production of a given text the authority to license alterations to that text, and as a result relegate compositor study and collation[23] to the textual apparatus rather than attempt to incorporate them into the text itself through emendation.

It seems to us that there is in fact no philosophical justification for emendation, which foregrounds the editor at the expense of the text. The distortions introduced by this process are all too readily incorporated into the text as holy writ. Macbeth's famous lines, for example, 'I dare do all that may become a man, / Who dares do more, is none,' on closer inspection turn out to be Rowe's. The Folio reads, 'I dare do all that may become a man, / Who dares no more is none.' There seems to us no pressing reason whatsoever to alter these lines,[24] and we prefer to confine all such editorial speculation to the critical apparatus. The worst form of emendation is conflation. It is now widely recognised that the texts of *M. William Shak-speare: his true chronicle historie of King Lear and his three daughters* (1608) and *The Tragedie of King Lear* (1623) differ so markedly that they must be considered as two distinct plays and that the composite *King Lear* which is reproduced in every twentieth-century popular edition of the play is a hybrid which grossly distorts both the originals from which it is derived. We believe that the case of *Lear* is a particularly clear example of a general proposition: that *whenever* distinct textualisations are conflated, the result is a hybrid without independent value. It should therefore go without saying that all the texts in this series are based upon single sources.

The most difficult editorial decisions we have had to face concern the modernisation of these texts. In some senses we have embarked upon a project of textual archaeology and the logic of our position points towards facsimile editions. These, however, are already available in specialist libraries, where they are there marginalised by those processes of cultural change which have rendered them alien and forbidding. Since we wish to challenge the hegemony of standard editions by circulating the texts within this series as widely as possible, we have aimed at 'diplomatic' rather than facsimile status and have modernised those orthographic and printing conventions (such as long s, positional variants of u and v, i and j, ligatures and contractions) which are no longer current and likely to confuse. We do so, however, with some misgiving, recognising that as a result certain possibilities open to the Elizabethan reader are thereby foreclosed. On the other hand, we make no attempt to standardise such features as speech prefixes and *dramatis personae*, or impose conventions derived from naturalism, such as scene divisions and locations, upon the essentially fluid and non-naturalistic medium of the Elizabethan theatre. In order that our own editorial practice should be as open as possible we provide as an appendix a sample of the original text in photographic facsimile.

GRAHAM HOLDERNESS AND BRYAN LOUGHREY

NOTES AND REFERENCES

1. The title page of the popular *Titus Andronicus*, for example, merely records that it was 'Plaide by the Right Honourable the Earle of Darbie, Earle of Pembrooke, and Earle of Sussex their Servants', and not until 1598 was Shakespeare's name attached to a printed version of one of his plays, *Love's Labour's Lost*.

2. For a stimulating discussion of the relationship between the three texts of *Hamlet*, see Steven Urkowitz, '"Well-sayd olde Mole", Burying Three *Hamlets* in Modern Editions', in Georgianna Ziegler (ed.), *Shakespeare Study Today* (New York: AMS Press, 1986), pp. 37–70.

3. In the year of Shakespeare's death Ben Jonson staked a far higher claim for the status of the playwright, bringing out the first ever collected edition of English dramatic texts, *The Workes of Beniamin Jonson*, a carefully prepared and expensively produced folio volume. The text of his Roman tragedy *Sejanus*, a play originally written with an unknown collaborator, was carefully revised to preserve the purity of authorial input. See Bryan Loughrey and Graham Holderness, 'Shakespearean Features', in Jean Marsden (ed.), *The Appropriation of Shakespeare: Post-Renaissance Reconstructions of the Works and the Myth* (Hemel Hempstead: Harvester Wheatsheaf, 1991), p. 183.

General Introduction

4. F. Madan and G.M.R. Turbutt (eds), *The Original Bodleian Copy of the First Folio of Shakespeare* (Oxford: Oxford University Press, 1905), p. 5.

5. Cited in D. Nicol Smith, *Eighteenth Century Essays* (Oxford: Oxford University Press, 1963), p. 48.

6. Margreta de Grazia, *Shakespeare Verbatim* (Oxford: Oxford University Press, 1991), p. 62. De Grazia provides the fullest and most stimulating account of the important theoretical issues raised by eighteenth-century editorial practice.

7. Unless the Hand D fragment of 'The Booke of Sir Thomas Moore' (British Library Harleian MS 7368) really is that of Shakespeare. See Stanley Wells and Gary Taylor, *William Shakespeare: A Textual Companion* (Oxford: Oxford University Press, 1987), pp. 461–7.

8. See Margreta de Grazia, 'The Essential Shakespeare and the Material Book', *Textual Practice*, vol. 2, no. 1 (Spring 1988).

9. Fredson Bowers, 'Textual Criticism', in O.J. Campbell and E.G. Quinn (eds), *The Reader's Encyclopedia of Shakespeare* (New York: Methuen, 1966), p. 869.

10. See, for example, Gary Taylor and Michael Warren (eds), *The Division of the Kingdoms* (Oxford: Oxford University Press, 1983).

11. Stanley Wells and Gary Taylor, *William Shakespeare: A Textual Companion* (Oxford: Oxford University Press, 1987), p. 2.

12. See, for example, Stanley Wells, 'Plural Shakespeare', *Critical Survey*, vol. 1, no. 1 (Spring 1989).

13. See, for example, *Textual Companion*, p. 69.

14. Thomas Platter, a Swiss physician who visited London in 1599 and recorded his playgoing; cited in *The Reader's Encyclopaedia*, p. 634. For a discussion of this passage see Richard Wilson, *Julius Caesar: A Critical Study* (Harmondsworth: Penguin, 1992), chapter 3.

15. E.K. Chambers, *The Elizabethan Stage* (Oxford: Oxford University Press, 1923), pp. 340–1.

16. The texts of the plays sometimes encode the kind of stage business Platter recorded. The epilogue of *2 Henry IV*, for example, is spoken by a dancer who announces that 'My tongue is weary; when my legs are too, I will bid you good night . . .'

17. Terence Hawkes, *That Shakespeherian Rag* (London, Methuen, 1986), p. 75.

18. For a discussion of Shakespeare's texts as dramatic scripts, see Jonathan Bate, 'Shakespeare's Tragedies as Working Scripts', *Critical Survey*, vol. 3, no. 2 (1991), pp. 118–27.

19. See, for example, Random Cloud [Randall McLeod], 'The Marriage of

Good and Bad Quartos', *Shakespeare Quarterly*, vol. 33, no. 4 (1982), pp. 421–30.

20. See, for example, Bryan Loughrey, 'Q1 in Modern Performance', in Tom Clayton (ed.), *The 'Hamlet' First Published* (Newark, University of Delaware Press, 1992) and Nicholas Shrimpton, 'Shakespeare Performances in London and Stratford-Upon-Avon, 1984–5', *Shakespeare Survey* 39, pp. 193–7.

21. *Textual Companion*, p. 60.

22. The concept of authorial intention, which has generated so much debate amongst critics, remains curiously unexamined within the field of textual studies.

23. Charlton Hinman's Norton Facsimile of *The First Folio of Shakespeare* offers a striking illustration of why this should be so. Hinman set out to reproduce the text of the original First Folio, but his collation of the Folger Library's numerous copies demonstrated that 'every copy of the finished book shows a mixture of early and late states of the text that is peculiar to it alone'. He therefore selected from the various editions those pages he believed represented the printer's final intentions and bound these together to produce something which 'has hitherto been only a theoretical entity, an abstraction: *the* First Folio'. Thus the technology which would have allowed him to produce a literal facsimile in fact is deployed to create an ahistorical composite which differs in substance from every single original upon which it is based. See Charlton Hinman, *The First Folio of Shakespeare* (New York, 1968), pp. xxiii–xxiv.

24. Once the process begins, it becomes impossible to adjudicate between rival conjectural emendations. In this case, for example, Hunter's suggestion that Lady Macbeth should be given the second of these lines seems to us neither more nor less persuasive than Rowe's.

Introduction

W H A T modern readers and audiences know as Shakespeare's *King Lear* is a composite construction formed by the merger of two distinct original texts, the First Quarto (Q1), *M. William Shakspeare: his true chronicle historie of the life and death of King Lear and his three daughters*, published in 1608; and *The Tragedie of King Lear*, published in the first collected edition of Shakespeare's plays, *Mr William Shakespeares Comedies, Histories, & Tragedies*, the First Folio of 1623 (F1). The two original printed texts are substantially different, with the Folio (F1) displaying short passages amounting to more than 100 lines of text which are not in the Quarto, and the latter (Q1) some 300 lines which are not in the Folio. Speeches are differently assigned; and there are more than 850 verbal variants. One whole 'scene' (that familiar from modern editions as 4.3, in which Kent and a 'Gentleman' discuss Cordelia's return from France) appears only in the Quarto, as do other significant moments such as the 'mock trial' of Gonorill and Ragan (this edition, p. 120), or Albany's powerful moral diatribe ('Tigers, not daughters') against Gonorill (p. 128).

I

M. William Shak-speare: his true chronicle historie of the life and death of King Lear and his three daughters has a unique history among the early printed texts that *Shakespearean Originals* sets out to recover, in that its reputation has in the last decade travelled all the way from various marginalising designations – 'Bad Quarto', memorial reconstruction, inaccurate copy from 'foul papers' – to authentication as a *bona fide* Shakespeare text, the initial formulation of a dramatic conception subsequently revised by Shakespeare himself into *The Tragedie of King Lear*. Thus *King Lear* is the only Shakespeare 'play' which is already, at the level of general publication, acknowledged as existing in more than one legitimate variant form. It is unnecessary therefore in the case of this text to argue a case either for its legitimacy as a text, or for its intrinsic interest as a textualisation. Unlike other texts in the series, *M. William Shak-speare: his true chronicle historie of the life and death of King Lear and his three daughters* has recently been published, either in modernised text or in photographic facsimile, in a number of different editions.[1]

These discrete publications of the Quarto version as a separate textualisation are welcome, and give some indication of the probable future shape of the standard Shakespeare text, and of the now unstandardised Shakespeare canon. They none the less remain, in the context of Shakespeare text-publishing, clearly marginal to the mainstream editorial tradition, which has since the early eighteenth century entailed a conflation of the two original texts, and which can still be found embodied in such dominant editions as those of the Arden Shakespeare (edited by Kenneth Muir, 1952, 1989) and the Penguin Shakespeare (edited by G.K. Hunter, 1972). Although the Arden Shakespeare is currently undergoing a major revision, R.A. Foakes will be contributing to its editorial totality yet another conflated text of '*King Lear*'.[2]

Introducing the current Arden edition of *King Lear*, Kenneth Muir distinguished the two original texts, in a familiar polarisation, as derived respectively from an authorial manuscript (1623) and a reconstruction by actors (1608):

> There is now fairly general agreement that the Folio text is not only more accurately printed, but also much nearer to what Shakespeare wrote, than that of the Quarto . . . it is generally accepted that Q is substantially inferior to F, and that the latter must therefore serve as the basis of a modern text.[3]

In fact twentieth-century textual studies have exhibited considerably more disagreement than is here suggested over the status of the 1608 version. It has been variously regarded as a Good Quarto (derived from an authorial manuscript), or as a Bad Quarto, derived by report from a performance.[4] Scholars who believed the text to have been reported also, however, felt that since it approximated more consistently than other comparable Bad Quartos to its 1623 counterpart, it was not perhaps in some ways 'bad' enough legitimately to earn the questionable designation of Bad Quarto.

W.W. Greg suggested[5] that if the text had derived from performance, it must have been directly transcribed by shorthand. Subsequently, however, G.I. Duthie argued[6] that no system of shorthand capable of such transcription existed in 1608, and that the quarto text must therefore have been reconstructed from memory. The memorial reconstruction theory normally postulates reconstruction by particular actors, on the grounds that their parts appear more accurately represented than those pertaining to other roles.[7] Although such an attribution did not appear to be an interpretative option in the case of the 1608 *Lear* text, exponents of the memorial reconstruction hypothesis remained undaunted. Alice Walker[8] adroitly inverted the normal criteria underpinning the theory, arguing that reconstruction could be attributed to the boy actors playing Gonorill and Ragan, since their parts appear *less* accurately 'reconstructed' than other parts of the play – the lads relying on memory to scribble down their own lines, but cribbing from the text to record those of others!

Duthie also displayed characteristic ingenuity in stretching the memorial reconstruction hypothesis to incorporate the atypical consistency of the 1608 text, by elaborating an engaging fantasy in which the text was reconstructed from memory by the whole cast. Since there is no marked discrepancy in point of approximation to the Folio text among the various roles, *all* the actors must perforce have been involved in reconstructing the text. Searching for a plausible set of circumstances in which the company might have wanted to undertake such an odd exercise, in a scenario worthy of Tom Stoppard, Duthie stranded a scriptless company of actors in the provinces, where they put the play together from memory as a team – 'during a provincial tour, the company having left the prompt-book (and the author's manuscript also, if the prompt-book was a transcript) in London'.[9] These examples illustrate the way in which the memorial reconstruction hypothesis, imaginatively liberated by the very iterability of the evidence, can become a purely theoretical game in which rules can be reconstructed without interrupting the course of play.[10]

II

Editorial practice continued to replicate the dominant bibliographical tradition, producing modern editions called simply '*King Lear*', and composed by merging the two original texts into a conflated composite. In 1975, the direction of the bibliographical debate began to change, when Michael Warren submitted a paper to the American Modern Language Association's journal (*PMLA*), discussing the relationship between two early texts of *King Lear*. While the traditional practice of editors had been to combine the two texts, so that all of the available material was united into a single entity, Warren suggested an alternative possibility, arguing that the two texts represented distinct, independent versions of the play, and that between them Shakespeare had systematically revised it. Far from having only one *King Lear*, we actually have two, each of equal authority.

Warren's paper was not well received in 1975. *PMLA* rejected it; a report on the article from one of the journal's readers concluded: 'This paper ought not to be published anywhere.' Within five years, however, Steven Urkowitz was advancing a similar argument in his 1980 book *Shakespeare's Revision of King Lear*.[11] Urkowitz was supported not just by Warren, but also by a group of other Shakespeare scholars, including Gary Taylor, Peter Blayney and Randall McLeod. In 1982, Blayney further advanced the revisionist cause in his *The Texts of King Lear*[12] and the following year Taylor and Warren published, as co-editors, *The Division of the Kingdoms: Shakespeare's Two Versions of King Lear*[13] – a groundbreaking collection of essays, each drawing out different aspects of the 'two-text hypothesis'. The revisionist position then became established in a major edition of Shakespeare's works in 1986 when Gary Taylor and Stanley Wells, as joint general editors, elected to include separate texts of both versions of *King Lear* in the new edition of the Oxford *Complete Works*,[14] offering the reader both *The History of King Lear* (based on the 1608 Quarto text) and *The Tragedy of King Lear* (based on the 1623 Folio text). Wells declared

Introduction

subsequently, in an article in *New Theatre Quarterly*, that 'once the hypothesis of revision is accepted, conflation becomes a logical absurdity . . . I believe that the conflated text has had its day'.[15]

That the overall effect of the edition was unsettling is evidenced by the reaction which the *Complete Works* encountered on publication. David Bevington, who had himself acted as editor for one of the single volume texts of the Oxford edition, reviewed the project in *Shakespeare Quarterly*. While praising much of the work produced by Wells and Taylor, he professed himself disquieted by 'something that is now awesomely present on the textual scene: the phenomenon of indeterminate Shakespeare', and he opened his review with a parable and a plea:

> A few years ago, when Coca-Cola introduced its ill-starred new Coke with considerable fanfare announcing to a skeptical world that the time had come for a big change, a *New York Times* reporter asked a man on the streets of Atlanta (where Coca-Cola is head-quartered) what he thought of the idea. 'They done fixed something that warn't broke!' was his memorable way of putting what so many devoted customers felt. And it pretty well expresses what this devoted reader of Shakespeare feels about the revisionist parts of the new Oxford Shakespeare . . . Coca-Cola soon admitted its mistake and brought back Classic Coke. Let us hope that the Oxford Press, which has presided so long and with such dignity over the concept of the standard author, will sooner or later bring back Classic Shakespeare.[16]

While the Wells and Taylor volume was indeed innovatory and provocative, the one thing it emphatically did not call into question was Bevington's cherished 'concept of the standard author'. Wells and Taylor may well have effected a distancing of their readers from certain aspects of individual texts, but the centrality of 'Shakespeare' to the entire enterprise was in no way questioned. In fact, if anything, the final effect was to extend to Shakespeare an even greater centrality than he had ever before possessed.

In practice textual revisionism acknowledges textual multiplicity as a fact, only to reconcile it with the integrity of the author. It can be accepted, since there are two *King*(s) *Lear*, that Shakespeare did not after all write only one, as long as it is admitted that he wrote both.

Introduction

The texts are different, as two children of different ages and the same parentage may differ: but both issue from the same parental source. In the opening decades of the present century, the 'New Bibliographers', drawing on theories of textual transmission developed in the realm of biblical studies by scholars such as Karl Lachmann, foregrounded a narrative of textual history which posited a stable, coherent authorial text which had been 'corrupted' in the process of entering the printed state. For New Bibliography the answer to the problem of the dispersal of a work over several different incarnations was to reduce this multiplicity to uniformity, by privileging one incarnation, that which appeared to approximate most nearly to the authorial original, and subordinating the others to it. From the late 1970s onwards the hegemony of the New Bibliography was systematically challenged by the proponents of revisionism, who (in theory, at least) rejected the conflation of many texts into a single compounded 'edition'. They proposed the separating out of individual textualisations, suggesting that such variations (or, at least some of them) may reflect distinct versions of a given text.

But, as Margreta de Grazia and Peter Stallybrass have noted with regard to the entire revisionist project in a recent valuable article: 'The recognition of multiple texts and variant passages is compromised by a theory of revision that ends up unifying and regulating what it had dispersed and loosened: all intertextual and intratextual variants are claimed in the name of a revising Shakespeare.'[17] De Grazia and Stallybrass further note that, within the revisionist framework, 'each multiple text constitutes a canon in miniature in which the author's personal and artistic development can be charted from revision to revision'.[18] David Bevington's fears notwithstanding, then, it is clear that what Warren, Urkowitz, Wells and Taylor and other revisionists present is by no means an 'indeterminate Shakespeare', since in revision theory Shakespeare becomes something very like a *determining principle*, a guarantor of authority and meaning – the fixed and stable point through which a clear relationship among multiple texts can be drawn.

The coherence of this authorial construction is of course guaranteed more by cultural and institutional than by bibliographical conditions. If the differentiation of texts into multiplicity occurs

[18]

within a cultural project framed by the author-function, then any rediscovered polyvocality will quickly be assimilated to an authorial monotone. The editorial strategy implied by the Oxford Shakespeare's radically disembodied *Lears* derives from a convergence of theatrical influence and textual plurality and in its logical conclusion points well beyond the constricting problematic of the institutional context – the 'Oxford Shakespeare' – within which it was developed. Ideological commitment to that totalising authorial project entails a deprioritising of the texts as we find them in history: discrete, mutually independent, overdetermined by particular conditions of cultural production – prior to (and also of course subsequent to) the editorial establishment of a canon in 1623. The radical theoretical possibilities released by a recognition of textual plurality, involving the deconstruction of the mainstream editorial tradition and an archaeological excavation of the 'real foundations' of that cultural edifice – the earliest printed texts themselves – become suppressed within the determining framework of an authorial construction. A theoretical move that could potentially return the texts to history and free them from the ideological constrictions of a canonical reproduction, loses its strategic mobility as the texts themselves are implicitly reconnected to the patriarchal source, silently reinscribed within the ideological problematic of an authoritarian cultural apparatus. Revision theory, even in its new theatrically inflected form of a directorial 'para-text' putatively supplied by Shakespeare, can still reconcile evidence of plurality between texts within the conceptual stability of an alternative author-function. Matthew Arnold's serenely detached master of a ready perfected poetic speech is replaced by Wells and Taylor's restlessly revising, theatrically engaged perfectionist playwright.[19]

The Oxford editors have made it clear, by deriving their individual play-texts from single sources, by printing alternative texts of *King Lear*, and by confessing to some degree of regret that the project could not in this respect have been more ambitious, that they acknowledge a wider applicability for the general principle of textual plurality. But since that aspiration remains firmly located within the hypothesis of authorial revision, it points not towards the liberation of texts from canonical colonisation and authorial sovereignty, but towards the juxtaposition of multiple texts reinscribed into a relationship of parallelism and reciprocal inter-dependence. 'I should like to see,' says Stanley Wells, 'double editions of all other plays where there are significant differences between the early witnesses to the texts.'[20] Ideally, then, a reader or performer should be offered not a multiplicity of *discrete texts*, but an opportunity to compare an early with a revised version, or an authorial draft with a theatrically adapted script. Texts in this model are related not to historical conditions of production and contexts of cultural appropriation, but to one another, and to their 'onlie begetter', the author.[21]

This problematic clearly acknowledges the influence of other determining factors, especially those involved in theatrical realization: but the final explanation of a text's mobility is located not in theatre or history or cultural context, but in the controlling mastery of authorial intention. The *Textual Companion* to the Oxford Shakespeare defines the processes of canonisation in a biological metaphor which invokes the operations of nature rather than the constructions of artifice. A play, like a child, is the product of two parents, 'born of the fruitful union of a unique author and a unique society'. Careful to acknowledge the limits of authorial mastery, the editors none the less elaborate here a metaphorical fantasy which validates a rigid and exclusive conception of authorial canon as an ideological totality:

> Like children, works of art acquire a being independent of those who conceived them. We may judge and interpret and enjoy a poem or person, without knowing the author or the father. But poems, like persons, come in families . . . In this sense a 'Complete Works' is the literary equivalent of a family reunion, the gathering of a clan of siblings . . . In recognizing the existence of such literary families, we need not accept any exaggerated theoretical estimate of the power of one parent – the 'author' – to impose successfully and consistently his or her intentions upon the children: we simply accept that each parent had some influence, often unconscious, commonly unpre-dictable, upon the maturing of each individual creation.[22]

However prudently hedged about with qualifications, the metaphor remains questionable in its privileging of a particular socio-logical form of the family, one that was indeed in Shakespeare's time only in the process of historical formation. Patrilinear, consanguineous, formed from the creative coupling of a clearly identified father ('Shakespeare') with a vacuous female other ('society'), tightly sealed in its legal definition of membership, a particular ethnocentric conception of family structure is here hypostasised as universal. The metaphor operates to contain an appropriate interest in the diversity of offspring within a set of deeply conservative editorial assumptions – all texts receive their signature of legitimacy from the authorial father; qualifications for membership, based on a community of blood, must be decided by an attestation of legitimate title; bastard offspring (such as Bad Quartos) are firmly placed outside the parameters of the family structure.

The textual scholar, who appears here in the guise of a family solicitor or real-estate lawyer, can prosecute his business of determining composition and inheritance, secure in the conviction that the canonical family is a formation of nature, not a construction of art. When Heminge and Condell, dedicating *Mr William Shakespeares Comedies, Histories, & Tragedies*, offered the plays to the patronage of the Earls of Pembroke and Montgomery – 'We have but collected them, and done an office to the dead, to procure his orphanes, Guardians' – they were invoking, in the same metaphor as the Oxford editors, an illuminatingly different historical form of the family.

III

The same controlling idea of authorial legitimation applies equally to an even more radical editorial initiative, Michael Warren's *The Complete 'King Lear' 1608–1623* (1989).[23] Where the Oxford editors printed only two separate texts, 1608 and 1623, the latter published no fewer than four separate texts: two Quartos (1608 and its 1619 reprint) and the Folio (1623) (each of these in an unbound, loose-leaf format, and individually boxed); together with a bound parallel text of F1 and Q1. Margreta de Grazia and Peter Stallybrass, in the article cited above, celebrate Warren's *Complete 'King Lear' 1608–1623* as the apotheosis of textual multiplicity: 'for over two hundred years, *King Lear* was one text; in 1986, with the Oxford Shakespeare, it became two; in 1989, with *The Complete 'King Lear' 1608–1623*, it became four (at least)'.[24] Progress is no longer measured retrospectively, as it was in the editorial culture initiated by the eighteenth-century scholars, and reconfirmed by New Bibliography, as a slow and gradual approximation to the *authorial* original; but prospectively, by the degree to which the modern edition can be seen splitting into modern textual forms correspondent to the original individually printed texts. While the Oxford Shakespeare's acknowledgement of two discrete texts of *'King Lear'* is posited by de Grazia and Stallybrass as the editorial break-through, they welcome Michael Warren's unbinding of *'King Lear'* into numerous discrete texts for its celebration of textual multiplicity. Warren's resolution of textuality into distinct original constituents is perceived as merely preparatory to a full-blown deconstructionist dispersal of all textual elements – books, pages, lines, words – into raw textual material, wide open to contemporary appropriation, de- and reconstruction:

> Facsimiles confer a sanctity upon the particulars of the duplicated text, hypostasising forms that were quite fluidly variable at their publication . . . Michael Warren's *The Complete 'King Lear' 1608–1623* designedly resists this arrest by opening up the textual proliferation that was endemic to early modern printing practices.[25]

Just as in the normal processes of early modern publication such texts were altered in the course of printing and before being finally bound, so the modern post-structuralist reader can freely manipulate the textual elements of the various texts to form any number of differential versions.

> The collected facsimiles of Warren's *The Complete 'King Lear'* open up a vastly wider range of textual possibility within the seventeenth century itself, both among different printings and among different formes of the same printing. Its three unbound *Lears* (Q1, Q2, and F1), each succeeded by either uncorrected or corrected pages, allows, indeed coaxes, the reader to assemble any number and combination of pages.[26]

A number of reservations need to be entered at this point. While Michael Warren *packages* his texts in a novel way, the fundamental principle governing the project is little different from the New Bibliographic/revisionist orthodoxy which de Grazia and Stallybrass attack with such acuity elsewhere in their article. Warren gathers his diverse texts under the rubric of a single entity (the singular *Complete 'King Lear'*), quite literally enclosing them together in a box. The individual texts are thus constelled around a single centre – no longer, perhaps, explicitly the revising author, but still the metacategory of 'the [singular] play', of which each actual published text is merely a part.

Furthermore, while Warren's edition clearly reflects 'the textual proliferation that was endemic to early modern printing practices', Paul Werstine has noted a distinctly contrary tendency in the parallel text volume which forms part of his box of texts. 'In the parallel-text facsimile,' Werstine observes, 'some agent has intervened by altering the photographs of F1 . . . the rules have been stripped from the F1 columns and gray space has been added so that their width seems to match that of the Q1 pages.'

> The visual effect is to stabilize both texts in opposition to each other and thus to endow each with a specious integrity. Consequently the photographs provide a visual analogue to the argumentative strategy of the revisionists, which has been to stabilize the texts by constructing mutually exclusive readings of Q1 and F1 and then logocentrically projecting these readings back onto Shakespeare as his differing but complete intentions for *King Lear*.[27]

The real point of attraction of Warren's presentation of his materials for de Grazia and Stallybrass seems to lie in the fact that within the greater box that is the *Complete 'King Lear'*, there can be found three smaller boxes containing unbound facsimiles of Q1, Q2 and F1. The enclosing walls of the box-within-a-box notwithstanding, the decision to print these texts in a loose-leaf format is taken as indicative of a metaphorical unbinding of the text, an opening up of the text to the free play of assemblage or disassemblage, subverting (in Foucault's terms) the tendency of the authorial principle to impede the 'free circulation, decomposition, and recomposition of fiction'.[28] The loose-leaf format 'allows, indeed coaxes, the reader to assemble any number and combination of pages' – to make and remake, one supposes, his or her own *Lear*(s). Quite how the reader is enabled to construct unilateral textualisations from printed pages – which by virtue of their material technology explicitly resist such manipulation, holding their words, sentences and paragraphs firmly in linear sequence – is not exactly clear.

[23]

Introduction

IV

The next publication of Q1 as a discrete text, *'King Lear': A Parallel-Text Edition*, edited by René Weis (1993) also derives its theoretical credentials from revision theory, and again links the two original texts inextricably together within the greater metacategory of 'Shakespeare's *King Lear*'. 'The most uncontroversial and perhaps the most sensible position to adopt about the two *Lears* is to submit that they are two states of the play, and that all the material they contain is by Shakespeare.'[29] This assumption justifies publishing the two original texts in facing-page parallel form, signalling that each is a separable element of a greater whole, and drawing attention to the similarities and differences between them. Parallel-text presentation is actually only one step away from conflation, since although the discrete texts are discriminated, they are separated out only to the extent of a double page, still held firmly together, and fixed into an inescapably comparative relationship with one another. Indeed Weis explicitly salutes the traditional conflated editions that her own publication might be understood to supersede:

> While it seems unlikely that a conflated text of *Lear* can in the future form a satisfactory basis for discussion, conflated *Lears* (as currently available in a number of excellent single editions by Muir 1989 and Hunter 1972, and in prestigious complete Shakespeares such as the Alexander, Riverside and Bevington texts) will undoubtedly continue to inspire readers and audiences.[30]

Weis is clearly so concerned to establish a diplomatic compromise with editorial peers that she hardly seems to notice the elitism of that suggestion that, while specialist academics will henceforth need separate texts, readers and audiences (who presumably don't engage in 'discussion') can continue to put up with traditional conflated versions.

Weis, in practice, adheres very closely to the principles of the mainstream editorial tradition: her texts are modernised, collated with reprints, and emended by reference to each other. Both are divided into acts and scenes, though in the original publications F is so divided, and Q isn't. Speech-headings are regularised ('EDMUND is substituted for '*Bastard*'); stage directions are filled out or even interpolated (where Q gives '*a letter*', and F no direction at all, both

[24]

Weis texts show ['*Gives Gloucester a letter*']). Q is not given its original title, but printed under the title invented by the Oxford editors, *The History of King Lear* – a title which, balancing exactly with the Folio's *The Tragedy of King Lear*, again confers on the two texts a perfect though quite inappropriate symmetry, 'stabilising' (in Paul Werstine's useful phrase) 'both texts in opposition to each other'.

V

An even more recent, and particularly significant, development is the publication, as part of the New Cambridge Shakespeare, of a single-volume edition of *M. William Shak-speare: his true chronicle historie of the life and death of King Lear and his three daughters*, edited by Jay L. Halio, under the title *The First Quarto of 'King Lear'*. This publication represents a significant departure from the norms of revisionist practice, since the text is not only incorporated into the Shakespeare canon (a move effected by the Oxford edition, and by the editions of Warren and Weis) but published individually as a discrete text; discriminated from the standard series format by a separate sub-series title (*Shakespeare: the Early Quartos*), but none the less accorded a place within the great Shakespearean whole.

Brian Gibbons, General Editor of the New Cambridge Shakespeare, provides a preface to this *Early Quartos* sub-series, indicating a rationale for the inclusion of such 'abbreviated', 'reported' or 'playhouse adaptation' quarto texts: 'These early quartos are not chosen as copy-texts for modern critical editions and are not readily available, though indispensable to advanced students of Shakespeare and of [sic] textual bibliography.'[31] The volume editor Jay L. Halio cites, as his theoretical credentials, revision theory and the 'two-text hypothesis':

> This edition of *King Lear* has been designed as a complementary text to the Folio-based edition published in the New Cambridge Shakespeare . . . this edition accepts the two-text hypothesis; indeed, that hypothesis is the main justification for bringing it to print.[32]

As we have seen, the usual justification for a discrete textualisation of Q1 is precisely that assumption of Shakespearean authorship of texts hitherto generally regarded as derived from performance and

Introduction

piracy. *Shakespeare: the Early Quartos* evidently, however, intends, with its explicit programme for reproducing a series of 'early quartos', including that of *King Henry V* – i.e. the notoriously Bad Quarto of 1600[33] – either to depart from the revisionist authorial problematic, or (presumably) to extend the claims of Shakespearean authorship to texts hitherto regarded as lying outside those authorial parameters. If it is the former ambition that is being advanced, then in its choice of texts for reproduction *Shakespeare: the Early Quartos* shares a rationale with *Shakespearean Originals*, which is that of prioritising the texts themselves over speculation as to their 'authorship' or cultural progenesis. Whether this methodological concurrence reflects an independent journey to the same theoretical point, or a more direct indebtedness to the earlier series, neither is anywhere explicitly acknowledged.[34]

The text presented in *The First Quarto of 'King Lear'* on the other hand, bears no resemblance to this *Shakespearean Originals* edition or to the original text itself. The text is wholly modernised and regularised, with the original format relineated and repunctuated according to principles established by modern editions of conflated or 'good' texts. Further, although Q1 is used as copy-text for the edition, Halio does not hesitate to emend it, quite unnecessarily and quite inconsistently, by reference to the Folio! Lear's opening speech in the first scene offers to the reader, brought up on standard conflated texts, a hybrid of the familiar and the strange:

> The map there. Know, we have divided
> In three our kingdom, and 'tis our fast intent
> To shake all cares and business of our state
> Confirming them on younger years.
>
> (1.1.31–4)

This certainly looks different from the standard Folio-based or conflated edition (exemplified here by Muir's Arden text):

> Give me the map there. Know that we have divided
> In three our kingdom; and 'tis our fast intent
> To shake all cares and business from our age,
> Conferring them on younger strengths . . .
>
> (1.1.36–9)

But it also differs from Q1 itself, as presented in this edition:

[26]

> The map there; know we have divided
> In three, our kingdome; and tis our first intent,
> To shake all cares and busines of our state,
> Confirming them on yonger yeares . . .
>
> (p. 72)

Halio's editing of these lines seems to me inexplicable. The Quarto reads 'first intent', but that reading is here in the Cambridge text corrected to the Folio's 'fast intent'. Conflated editions normally prefer F's readings, privileging 'conferring', 'years' and 'of our state' over the alternatives offered by the Quarto. But why should 'fast' be preferred to 'first', even by the criteria and principles of conflation? If this purports to be an edition of Q1 rather than a conflated text, what justification can there be for 'correcting' the perfectly legitimate 'first'? Or do we find in this slippage the trace of a symptomatic instinctive preference for what is assumed to have been the 'fast [settled, determined] intent' of the author, over the 'first intent' possibly to be found embodied in the Quarto text?

Other forms of editorial intervention such as relineation draw on a long editorial tradition: the textual apparatus is liberally sprinkled with citations of eighteenth-century editors such as Pope and Rowe. Kent's lines in the first scene

> What wilt thou doe ould man, think'st thou that dutie
> Shall have dread to speake, when power to flatterie bowes,
> To plainnes honours bound when Majesty stoops to folly.
> Reverse thy doome, and in thy best consideration
> Checke this hideous rashnes . . .
>
> (This edition, p. 75)

is relineated by Halio thus:

> What wilt thou do, old man?
> Thinks't thou that duty shall have dread to speak
> When power to flattery bows? To plainness honour's bound,
> When majesty stoops to folly. Reverse thy doom,
> And in thy best consideration check
> This hideous rashness.

on the authority of Johnson's relineation of the Folio text. The objective seems to be to produce regular decasyllabic 'pentameter' lines out of the apparent 'irregularity' of the original. Yet Johnson's version still contains 'irregular' lines of 12 or 13 syllables ('When

[27]

power . . .' and 'When majesty . . .'); and in order to win a couple of 'regular' lines ('Think's thou . . .' and 'And in thy best . . .'), the syntactical structure of Kent's 'plain' speech, exemplified by the straightforward one-line statement that lies in the original at the heart of his speech – 'To plainnes honours bound when Majesty stoops to folly' – has been distorted into the more sophisticated enjambement of the modernised text. Why should a modern editor want to adopt an eighteenth-century editor's strategies of 'improvement', unless of course the general Augustan cultural policy of improvement through alteration is also, perhaps unconsciously, still being pursued?

Halio's text employs, albeit in parenthesis, the familiar stage directions interpolated by eighteenth-century editors – '*Aside*' for 'What shall Cordelia do?', '*Gives him a letter*', '*Strikes him*', and so forth. Act and scene divisions, introduced in the Folio and standardised by the editorial tradition, but notably absent from the Quarto, are also included. Speech-headings are not those of the Quarto, most strikingly in the consistent conversion of '*Bastard*' to 'EDMUND'.

VI

In the text presented here, at least, the whoreson is acknowledged. This *Shakespearean Originals* edition publishes the text of *M. William Shak-speare: his true chronicle historie of the life and death of King Lear and his three daughters*, separated from its younger sibling, and for the first time since 1608, under its original title. That title, whoever composed and attached it to the text, calls attention precisely to some of the differences between the two originals. By contrast with the austere *The Tragedie of King Lear*, which seeks to contain the text within a distinct genre, Q's title invokes a more diverse generic background, claiming the play for serious historiography ('true . . . history'), more legendary modes of historiography ('true chronicle') and fairy-tale (*King Lear and his three daughters*). In that character of generic diversity (common to both original texts but in some ways more manifest in Q), and not in a changing of authorial mind, lies the basis of their textual volatility.

In keeping with its generic diversity, the narrative origins of the Lear-plays disclose an extraordinary variety, which in turn influenced subsequent reproduction of the play in the post-Restoration theatre. If a modern reader or playgoer, familiar with the various printed and performance texts that go under the aggregate title of 'Shakespeare's *King Lear*', were able to travel back in time to see a production of that play in a theatre any time between 1681 and 1823, he or she would undoubtedly receive something of a shock. Not only would the language of the play seem entirely rewritten: even the basic plot would be found radically dissimilar to the familiar Shakespearean action. During that 142-year period, Cordelia's reluctance to marry did not remain a mystery: she was already in love, with Edgar. There was no trace of the Fool, a central figure for modern criticism of the play. Above all, our time-travelling spectator would be astonished to discover that the play was no longer a tragedy: that within 73 years of its original publication in 1608, it had acquired a happy ending. Cordelia and Edgar manage between them to defeat the powers of the older daughters, and to restore Lear to his throne.

Neither Lear nor Cordelia die in this version. Cordelia was instead rescued, first from rape and then from hanging, by her lover Edgar. The play ends with Edgar renouncing any claim he might as victor have over the kingdom, preferring to join Cordelia in a romantic retirement. The closing lines of the play – familiar to us from modern editions as Edgar's –

> The weight of this sad time we must obey;
> Speak what we feel, not what we ought to say.
> The oldest hath borne most: we that are young
> Shall never see so much, nor live so long.[35]

for a century and a half reappeared in a radically altered form, though still spoken (as in the 1623 edition) by Edgar:

> Our drooping country now erects her head,
> Peace spreads her balmy wings, and Plenty blooms.
> Divine Cordelia, all the gods can witness
> How much thy love to empire I prefer!
> Thy bright example shall convince the world
> (Whatever storms of Fortune are decreed)
> That truth and virtue shall at last succeed.[36]

'Succeed' hints there at a double meaning, with the primary sense 'emerge with success' further suggesting 'inherit power by succession'. This play could be described as a political romance, concluding as it did with a particular kind of happy ending, entailing the restoration of a previously abdicated monarchy.

This version of *King Lear*, which completely replaced the Shakespearean version in the theatre during the whole of that period, was written by Nahum Tate, a popular poet and dramatist who later became Poet Laureate. It was standard practice in this period to regard Shakespeare's plays as texts to be adapted and rewritten, indeed virtually translated into what was considered the more polished and civilised language of the day. From the perspective of the later seventeenth century, Elizabethan drama appeared to be the product of a relatively uncivilised culture, strong on genius and imagination, short on taste and correctness. To a writer like Tate, the dramatic writings of that earlier period seemed works of pure 'Nature' – 'a Heap of Jewels, unstrung and unpolisht – dazling in their disorder'[37] – and the modern poet's job was therefore to polish and restring the stones into an orderly configuration. But even in such a context, where free adaptation was regarded as an appropriate way of reproducing earlier texts, Tate's alteration of '*King Lear*' from tragedy to comedy, and the strikingly long period of currency and popularity enjoyed by that adaptation, still seem remarkable.

The most obvious change introduced is that of the happy ending, which helps to convert the dramatic action from tragedy to romance: from a narrative in which innocence and weakness are mercilessly punished along with the guilty, to one in which virtue and proper sentiment are rewarded with romantic reconciliation and the restoration of legitimacy. Despite the contemporary popularity and esteem accorded Tate's adaptation (Dr Johnson preferred it to Shakespeare's), in modern criticism it has been ridiculed as a travesty of Shakespeare – 'notorious', 'infamous'. 'Tate's Lear', said Maynard Mack, 'invites ridicule, and deserves it'.[38] Such a view is perhaps inescapable if we compare the versions, as our playgoing time-traveller compared them, in historical retrospect, with the Shakespearean drama taken as the 'original' of which Tate's adaptation was a corruption, the norm from which Tate manifestly deviated.

Introduction

This is not, however, the only way of looking at it. Shakespeare did not invent the 'King Lear' story. It was, on the contrary, a traditional historical legend with a long ancestry, existing in a large number of different retellings, some of them in Shakespeare's time relatively recent. The versions of the story most likely to have influenced the 1608 and 1623 dramatic versions are (i) the reign of Lear recounted as part of the history of early Britain in Holinshed's *Chronicles*; (ii) the story as narrated in Book 2 of Spenser's *The Faerie Queene*; and (iii) an anonymous play entitled *The True Chronicle Historie of King Leir*, performed in the 1590s and published in 1605. The most striking feature of these different legendary and historical narratives, from the perspective of a comparison between Shakespeare and Tate, is that all these versions tell the same story as Tate's adaptation. The 'King Lear' story is a historical romance narrative of restoration, in all versions but those exemplified by the two Shakespearean texts. It is so in Holinshed's version:

> Herevpon, when this armie and nauie of ships were readie, Leir and his daughter Cordeilla with hir husband tooke the sea, and arriuing in Britaine, fought with their enimies, and discomfited them in battle . . . and then was Leir restored to his kingdome, which he ruled after this by the space of two yeeres, and then died, fortie yeeres after he first begun to reigne.[39]

And in Spenser's:

> The wretched man gan then auise too late,
> That loue is not, where most it is profest,
> Too truely tryde in his extreamest state;
> At last resolu'd likewise to proue the rest,
> He to *Cordelia* to him selfe addrest,
> Who with entire affection him receau'd,
> As for her Syre and king she seemed best;
> And after all an army strong she leau'd,
> To war on those, which him had of his realme bereau'd.
>
> So to his crowne she him restored againe,
> In which he dyde, made ripe for death by eld,
> And after wild, it should to her remaine:
> Who peacably the same long time did weld:
> And all mens harts in dew obedience held.[40]

If Shakespeare's *King Lear* is taken as a starting-point, it appears

[31]

that Tate distorted the original (with what seems to modern witnesses quite inexplicable success), and that the original was then permanently restored to the theatre in the nineteenth century. When modern dramatists undertake similarly free adaptations of Shakespeare (a pertinent example would be Edward Bond's *Lear*), their rewritings do not replace the 'original', but parallel and complement it; the Shakespearean norm remains in place, to exercise a salutary and corrective influence on any manifest deviation. But Tate's adaptation took place when the play was a bare 73 years old, and when both the unassailable Shakespearean reputation, and the stable Shakespearean text, were yet to be consolidated (the first edition of Shakespeare's works – other than simple reprints of the 1623 Folio – that of Nicholas Rowe, was not published until 1709). Prior to Shakespeare's play, the 'King Lear' story existed as a particular historical narrative with a long history stretching from the Middle Ages to the early seventeenth century. Tate was, if anything, actually 'restoring' the 'Lear' story's original shape and generic character after its 'distortion' by Shakespeare.

This evidence provides a different way of looking at the same developmental process. During the greater part of its history, the 'Lear' story took the form of a historical romance ending in restoration. For a brief period between the first decade of the seventeenth century and 1681, the story appeared and achieved currency in the Shakespearean form, as a tragedy. It was then restored by Tate to its original romance form, in which it persisted until 1838. Thereafter, with the consolidation of Shakespeare's prominence as Britain's national dramatist, the Shakespearean version became accepted as the only fictionalisation of the 'Lear' story to retain any enduring artistic value.

The modern reader approaches this problem from a perspective predetermined by the location of Shakespeare's play as a fixed point of reference. But an attention to the broad field of cultural production from which the *King Lear* texts emanated would suggest that the Shakespearean dramatisations cannot be disentangled so easily from the narrative materials that went into their making. Narratives never exist as pure story; stories are always narrated. Narration confers upon a particular telling or retelling the characteristics of a specific genre, the shaping structure of a certain cultural convention, a guiding framework of cultural rules that enables the reader to orientate him- or herself in relation to the overall pattern and local details of the narrative. A narrative is never separable from its genre, from that particular configuration of conventions into which the story is located. The 'King Lear' story demonstrates a range of narrative possibilities, and in each manifestation the chosen convention is overtly foregrounded.

> Leir the son of Baldud was admitted ruler ouer the Britaines in the year of the world 3105 . . . (Holinshed)[41]

> He had three daughters, first and eldest hight *Gonerell*:
> Next after hir, my sister *Ragan* was begote:
> The thirde and last was, I the yongest namde *Cordell* . . . (Higgins)[42]

> I thought the King had more affected the Duke of *Albany* than *Cornwell* . . . (Shakespeare)[43]

Holinshed's perspective is that of the historical chronicle, impersonal, objective, matter-of-fact. John Higgins' first-person narrative foregrounds the folk-tale structure of the 'Lear' story, pointing up its distinct resemblance to archetypal fairy-tales such as that of Cinderella. The Shakespearean version plunges the spectator directly into a dramatised action already in progress.

The 'Lear' story thus manifested a range of narrative and generic capabilities before it emerged in the Shakespearean dramatisations. It could be narrated as historical romance, ending in restoration and unity; or it could be narrated, as it is in both Shakespearean texts, as tragedy, culminating in the deaths of Lear and Cordelia. The full historical legend contained both possibilities, which is why it could function as a source for such differential narrations. In the traditional versions, including those of Holinshed and Spenser, the romance history of Lear's restoration was followed by a tragic sequel. Lear survived his own restoration to sovereignty by only a few years. He was succeeded by Cordelia, who reigned for five years as 'supreme governesse of Britaine'. After her husband's death, her nephews (the sons of Gonorill and Ragen), 'disdaining to be under the government of a woman', rebelled against and imprisoned her. Cordelia was 'laid . . . fast in ward, wherewith she tooke such grief, being a woman of manlie courage, and despairing to recouer libertie, there she slue hirselfe'.[44] In Spenser's version Cordelia is less 'manlie', and hangs herself merely from 'weariness' of long imprisonment.[45] The tragic sequel to the traditional chronicle history was thus incorporated into the Shakespearean versions, though as assassination rather than suicide.

To a story already coloured by the genres of history, romance and tragedy were added elements of comedy – particularly the grotesque humour at work in the scenes of Lear's madness, a narrative element not to be found in any of the earlier versions. Hence both texts of the Shakespearean Lear-narrative manifest a strikingly diversified dramatic medium. It is axiomatic to traditional scholarship that this generic eclecticism and catholicity of sources, while typical of Shakespeare's method of working, does not unsettle the self-evident artistic unity of the final product. Whatever Shakespeare did to the structural pattern and figurative detail of the traditional 'Lear'-story must have been done for good reasons, since the status of the Shakespearean synthesis cannot be challenged. Kenneth Muir, for example, acknowledging some of the play's apparently dubious origins, none the less cannot wish the fault undone, the issue of it being so proper:

> It is likely that the old play [*The True Chronicle Historie of King Leir*] gave Shakespeare the idea of writing on King Lear; but he had long been familiar with the versions of Holinshed and Spenser, and also with *The Mirror for Magistrates*. As we have seen, he was cheerfully eclectic in his use of sources, combining details and phrases from each. On the one hand he rejected the happy ending of *King Leir*, and gave form to its formlessness; on the other hand he rejected the undramatic elements of the versions of Spenser, Holinshed, and Higgins, in which the defeat and the suicide of the heroine come as an epilogue irrelevant to the story of Lear himself. The suicide of Cordelia would have been intolerable to a sensitive audience, and her murder necessitated the punishment of the guilty: Goneril and Regan could not be suffered to escape, if Cordelia were to die; and Lear could not, without anti-climax, be restored to the throne. Out of a moral story with a happy ending and an irrelevant, despairing epilogue, Shakespeare created a homogeneous tragedy.[46]

It is abundantly clear from the sophistry of this argument that, in Muir's view, whatever Shakespeare did to the traditional Lear materials would have been justified in the outcome: he could not put a foot wrong. But why should a tragic reworking of a narrative of restoration be so obviously and inevitably superior to a romance version, and why should a pattern of restoration necessarily prove an anti-climax? Dr Johnson thought the romance of restoration superior to the tragedy, and Tolstoy found the *True Chronicle Historie of King Leir* less, not more, formless than Shakespeare's play. Why should the subsequent fate of Cordelia be deemed 'irrelevant' to the story of Lear, unless Lear's history can be conceived of without Cordelia? Why should the heroine's suicide be 'intolerable', and who says Shakespeare's theatre had a 'sensitive' audience? The traditional narrative is castigated as a 'moral story', yet Muir's own *Lear* is virtually a cautionary tale of guilt and inevitable punishment.

VII

The four most significant generic contexts influencing the Lear-plays are history, romance, comedy and tragedy. As a historical legend, the Lear-story acquired traces of a historiographical context that manifested themselves throughout the play-texts. As exemplified in Holinshed, the Lear-tale is a historical narrative of legitimacy, power, political authority and military struggle: a story of a kingdom divided, invaded and reunited. Though clearly the Lear-narrative is not historical in the same sense as a play like *The Life of Henry the Fift*, the texts none the less connect with seventeenth-century historiography, and remain available for historical reinterpretation. Thus modern critical studies like that of J.F. Danby,[47] which reads '*King Lear*' via a marxist understanding of early modern economic and political philosophies, or modern performance interpretations like the 1970 film version directed by Grigori Kozintsev, which explores the Lear-narrative as a grand historical epic of feudalism, have been able to present convincing renderings of the Lear-story as history. In the early seventeenth century that history was also, of course, a matter of myth and legend, and therefore available for reproduction in that contemporary political language that invoked 'mythical charters' of the past to legitimise and sanction modern configurations of power.[48]

Contingent upon the legendary dimensions of the Lear-tale was a strong element of romance, manifest in the versions of Spenser and *The True Chronicle Historie of King Lear*. Within the framework of a historical and political narrative that could be understood either diachronically, as reconstruction of the past, or anachronistically, as indicative of the present, the Lear-plays generate folk-tale and romance motifs of banishment and exile, recognition and return, disguise and mistaken identity. The courtly and romance language of the 'division' scene begins as ritualised ceremony, but slides unexpectedly into genuine pastoral discourse:

> Fairest *Cordelia* that art most rich being poore,
> Most choise forsaken, and most loved despisd,
> Thee and thy vertues here I ceaze upon,
> Be it lawful I take up whats cast away.
>
> (p. 78)

A fundamental romance archetype, the abandonment to chance of a royal child and her acceptance dowerless by a royal suitor, is enacted in the course of a few lines. Other romance elements include the story of Kent, a loyal courtier banished for honest speaking who re-enters his master's service in disguise; and the Gloster subplot, with the good brother disinherited by deception, disguised as a beggar until the time is ripe to return to single combat and the offer of a kingdom. A precursor of the play's climax, and a provisional fulfilment of its romance pattern (soon to be overtaken by tragic calamity), is figured in a reversion to the chivalric romance of the duel between Edgar (who appears, from nowhere, as the stereotypical anonymous challenger) and his brother Edmund.

The elements of comedy that appear so marked in the Lear-texts are not simply focused on the Fool, but dispersed across those figures who experience real or assumed madness, Edgar and Lear himself. G. Wilson Knight identified this characteristic in an essay usefully deploying terms such as 'grotesque' and 'absurd' to isolate the defining qualities of Lear-humour.[49] Knight's analysis reproduces these incongruities as tragicomedy: but a more modern understanding of the 'grotesque' would be prepared to acknowledge obviously satirical, and in many instances even saturnalian, energies of the plays. Verbal destabilisation of legitimate hierarchy

[36]

co-exists with fantasies of a world turned upside-down, authority overturned and the humble exalted:

> . . . see how yon Justice railes upon yon simple theefe, harke in thy eare handy, dandy, which is the theefe, which is the Justice, thou hast seene a farmers dogge barke at a begger . . . And the creature runne from the cur, there thou mightst behold the great image of authoritie, a dogge, so bade in office . . .
>
> (p. 137)

Throughout the 'storm-scenes', where the dramatic action presents an aristocratic clan forced to hovel with the wretched of the earth, we witness the enactment of such a grotesque comedy of subversion, facilitated by the 'topsy-turvey' wit of the Fool, and the 'handy, dandy' madness of the foolish king.

The '*King Lear*' plays locate themselves firmly into the typology of tragedy: and it is in this respect that the 'Shakespearean' Lear-texts resemble one another more closely than they resemble any of the other narrative versions. Neither of the two texts betrays any ambiguity on this point in narrative terms: Cordelia is executed, Lear dies. But the distinctive character of the Lear-tragedy is that in its contradictory relationship with its narrative sources, it is quite unlike any other 'Shakespearean' tragedy. If that distinctive willingness of the Shakespearean Lear-texts to read their sources against the grain introduces into the texts some residual conflict with the ancient lines of the romance-narrative, then even the ostensibly uncontroversial category of tragedy might become complicated and problematical. We already have two Lear-plays: but are there even within the space interpolated by this bifurcation further discrete Lear-narratives, locked in conflictual interplay?

While much discussion within the two-text debate, concerned as it has been to trace a trajectory of authorial alteration, has focused on speculative discriminations between different states of the texts' development, little attention seems to have been paid to possible correlations between the texts' significant divergences and their separate generic dimensions. Where the texts of the Lear-play, in other words, differ substantially one from another, it is likely to be along the axes of, or the sutures joining, those historical, romance, comic and tragic narrative influences that constitute their iterable and volatile textuality. This in fact is the case, and can be illustrated

[37]

briefly by reference to: differing treatments of the war, where one text clearly dramatises civil war and the other foreign invasion; separable representations of Cordelia's home-coming, in particular the inclusion in Q1 of the scene reporting Cordelia's return to Britain (this edition, p. 130); discrepant versions of the 'hovel-scene' which, in Q1 only, contains the 'mock trial' of Gonorill (this edition, p. 120); and the strikingly dissimilar versions of the final tragic conclusion.

VIII

In both texts Cordelia's return has the objective of intervening, in what is already a situation of violent civil discord, on behalf of the king and against the forces of her sisters. The issue of discrepancy between the texts centres on whether Cordelia brings a French army with her: whether, in other words, the pro-Lear alliance formed between Albany, Gloster (later Edgar), and Cordelia, involves the military intervention of a foreign power. '[T]her's a division betwixt the Dukes' says Gloster in both texts; but in Q1 this is followed by 'ther's part of a power already *landed*', where F1 gives 'already *footed*'. Q1 openly and consistently identifies the French army as a player in the action; where F1 with equal consistency omits such allusions, and throws the emphasis on internecine conflict and civil war. The relevant Q1 passages include:

> [*Gon.*] Wher's thy drum? *France* spreds his banners in our noyseles
>   land,
>   With plumed helme, thy state begins thereat
>   Whils't thou a morall foole sits still and cries
>   Alack why does he so?
>
>   (p. 129)

> [*Alb.*]   . . . for this busines
>   It touches us, as *France* invades our land
>   Not bolds the King . . .
>
>   (p. 144)

Neither of these references has any counterpart in F1. Where Kent initially broaches the prospect of open civil war, the texts diverge in the same way. Q1's version elaborates on the imminent French invasion:

[38]

> . . . there is division,
> Although as yet the face of it be cover'd,
> With mutual cunning, twixt *Albany* and *Cornwall*
> But true it is, from *France* there comes a power
> Into this scattered kingdome, who alreadie wise in our
> Have secret feet in some of our best Ports,   (negligence,
> And are at point to shew their open banner, . . .
>
> (p. 111)

While F1 reduces this to the ambiguous or evasive[50]

> There is diuision
> (Although as yet the face of it is couer'd
> With mutual cunning) 'twixt Albany, and Cornwall:
> Who haue, as who haue not, that their great Starres
> Thron'd and set high; Seruants, who seeme no lesse,
> Which are to France the Spies and Speculations
> Intelligent of our State.

The scene of Cordelia's return, which occurs only in Q1, reports the landing of a French army accompanied by both Cordelia and the French king, who then returns to France leaving his general 'Monsier *la far*' in charge.

These variations thus represent a substantive textual difference in each play's recycling of the historical Lear-legend. Earlier scholars suspected the influence of censorship, with Q1's representation of a foreign invasion toned down, on censorial instruction, to F1's domestic civil war. Greg thought the motif of foreign invasion presented a 'patriotic dilemma', suggesting that the nation could not save itself but had to be liberated by a foreign ally; and Madeleine Doran argued that the Folio made cuts in the Quarto text precisely to alter the nationality of Cordelia's military 'powers'.[51] The leading revisionists, however, have rejected this view, arguing that the diminution of France's role derives from 'an altered dramatic vision of the last half of the play'.[52] René Weis also agrees with this position, citing Taylor's suggestion that F produces 'a more benevolent impression, one more clearly personified by Cordelia herself', and concurring that the more benevolent version is the revised one, the one representing Shakespeare's ultimate intentions and considered judgement.[53]

All these arguments around censorship and revision remain

speculative and inconclusive, relying as they do on unproven assumptions about agency and development – that is, that an authorial agent (whether Shakespeare or others) deliberately modified Q1, in response either to externally imposed pressures of censorship or to internally generated possibilities of artistic reconstruction, to produce the 'revised' Folio text. Such arguments need working assumptions about the rationale for any general or particular change: and here these assumptions seem particularly questionable. Arguments from censorship assume the French invasion to have been, in Greg's words, a 'ticklish business'.[54] But why should the representation of civil war, in a play printed in 1608, have seemed more acceptable than that of foreign invasion? As Gary Taylor points out, the Jacobean administration had if anything far more to fear from the former than from the latter.[55] Equally, however, revisionist arguments have assumed that the depiction of a state healing its own civil discord by internal subjugation of injustice, presents a more 'benevolent' image than that of one requiring assistance from a foreign ally. This presupposes that such a healing process actually takes place: an assumption that seems to me to rest more securely on critical tradition than on anything that appears in the text.

These debates are none the less not without interest, acknowledging as they do the irreducible differences between discrete textualisations. My own preference is simply to shift the terrain of discussion away from speculation as to origins, and towards textual interpretation of the original documents. For example, the revisionist proposition that from the ambiguities of Q1, F1 consolidates a mature and benevolent tragic vision, can be seen to reinforce the reciprocity of the two texts as 'a canon in miniature',[56] enacting that classic Shakespearean trajectory, dear to critical tradition, from tragic despair to enlightened resignation. Some sacrifices are none the less entailed in this heroic scholarly rescuing of the integrity of authorial vision. An interpretation that emphasises the potentialities for internal national regeneration must place much more emphasis on the battered male survivors of the civil conflict – Albany, Edgar, Kent – than on Cordelia, the good daughter who reappears only to suffer defeat and ignominious death. But Cordelia's strength is defined in the Quarto very much in terms of the military power she brings with her and leads. In the battle scene (modern editions 5.2) Cordelia in Q1 is announced as leading both the French army and the British king: *Enter the powers of France over the stage, Cordelia with her father in her hand*. In F1 both the French presence and Cordelia's priority have been reduced: *Enter with drum and colours Lear, Cordelia and Soldiers over the stage*.

The revisionist arguments that express a preference for the Folio version's diminution of the French invasion entail a distinct complicity with both authorial intentionality and with a conservative critical agenda that invests its desires in the surviving male protagonists of the tragedy. The Quarto text more sharply and painfully foregrounds the incommensurable discrepancy between the promise of Cordelia's return, and its manifest failure, as both the heroine and her imported army endure defeat.

Another way of putting the distinction between differing representations of the war, would be to say that the geopolitical worlds of Q1 and F1 are equally incommensurable. The world of the Quarto text is more obviously the terrain of romance, where both geographical place and national boundaries are notoriously ambiguous and undefined. Value and significance are invested in the person and the cause, rather than in whatever territorial arrangements currently pertain; the plays do begin, after all, with the arbitrary division of a map along the lines of personal idiosyncracy and family preference. What is important in Q1 is not the nationality of the 'powers' Cordelia brings, but that she reappears empowered, as the potential saviour of the romance narrative. F1, we might say, has introduced into its geopolitics more modern sensitivities about national boundaries, mapping the integrity of the early modern nation-state onto the romance fluidity of Lear's Britain. In doing so, the text curtails some of the potencies available within chronicle romance to strengthen and centralise the representation of Cordelia.[57]

IX

The most substantial difference between Quarto and Folio texts concerns precisely this configuration of Cordelia, the French army and romance convention. The scene, familiar from conflated editions

[41]

as 4.3, in which Kent and a Gentleman discuss Cordelia's return from France, appears only in the Quarto text. The scene is virtually a preface to the following section in which Cordelia herself converses with a Doctor: Cordelia's return is therefore first reported and described before she herself appears to the audience. The convention of report allows for the full intensity of an iconographic idealisation of Cordelia, in which she is represented both sentimentally and heroically; a virtual force of passion, and a source of discipline and control; both dutiful daughter, and warrior queen:

> (of griefe.
> *Kent.* Did your letters pierce the queene to any demonstration
> *Gent.* I say she tooke them, read them in my presence,
> And now and then an ample teare trild downe
> Her delicate cheeke, it seemed she was a queene over her passion,
> Who most rebell-like, sought to be King ore her.
>
> (p. 130)

Although focused on powerful emotions, the text immediately draws analogies between person and state, individual feeling and political context. Cordelia is of course both monarch and rebel, not only in terms of her emotional control. She is also the daughter who 'most rebell-like' defiantly subverted the authority of the king. She is 'queene' of France but is here as a pretender, seeking political control over Britain; and therefore a 'rebell' to the legally consti-tuted (though manifestly unjust) authorities of the kingdom. She is out to restore a fallen king whose personal weakness corresponds in inverse ratio to her evident strength, a powerful queen hoping to prop up an enfeebled monarch. Metaphorically the 'passion' that is figured as a 'King' is also Lear himself, whose initial banishment of his daughter is thus formulated as a 'rebell-like' usurpation of true moral sovereignty.

The subtle play of this political vocabulary articulates a complex configuration of meanings around legitimacy, restoration, force and authority. In the following scene Cordelia attempts to clarify her cause by disentangling these ambiguous valencies:

> *Mes.* News Madam, the Brittish powers are marching hither-
> *Cord.* Tis knowne before, our preparation stands,   (ward.
> In expectation of them, ô deere father

It is thy busines that I go about, therfore great *France*
My mourning and important teares hath pitied,
No blowne ambition doth our armes in fight
But love, deere love, and our ag'd fathers right . . .

(p. 132)

In dutiful compliance with her romance heritage, Cordelia here offers 'love' as a transcendent value, occluding the political and military motives attaching to her mission. Where the Gentleman's metaphors invest Cordelia with an aura of power that is both impressive and dangerous, she herself explicitly disavows any 'rebell-like' intentions, reassuring the audience that this is no act of territorial aggression, but a mission of mercy, a crusade of liberation. The military power of France is merely an adjunct to the irenic aspiration of Cordelia's filial duty; indeed the military commitment itself is initially motivated by compassion rather than anger:

. . . great *France*
My mourning and important teares hath pitied . . .

(p. 132)

It is no reflection on the purity of Cordelia's represented motives to observe that the balance of moral and political values in her language presents genuine difficulties. The familiar routine characterisation of every historical invasion as a necessary act of liberation, and the perennial human effort to confer a pacific sanction on military violence, render no less problematical the effort visible here to subjugate passionate indignation to the discipline of a serene patience. In Cordelia's behaviour, as depicted by the Gentleman, we witness a powerful struggle between compassion and rage:

Faith once or twice she heav'd the name of father,
Pantingly forth as if it prest her heart,
Cried sisters, sisters, shame of Ladies sisters:
Kent, father, sisters, what ith storme ith night,
Let pitie not be beleeft there she shooke,
The holy water from her heavenly eyes,
And clamour moystened her, then away she started,
To deale with griefe alone.

(p. 131)

The linguistic violence visible and audible here in those strong

[43]

verbs – 'heav'd', 'prest', 'shooke' – testifies to a suppressed anger that is sharply at odds with the image of tearful feminine sympathy. Even the 'holy water from her heavenly eyes' joins with the more demonstrative 'clamour' to mollify ('moysten') her righteous indignant anger. Just as in the play's opening scene Cordelia's silence was used as a sharp-edged weapon, so here she does not retreat into private grief, but actively 'start[s]' aside in order to master her own emotions, 'To deale with griefe alone'.

The reporting Gentleman remains committed to a project of idealisation that disallows the presence within Cordelia's emotional range of that violence of anger that so pervades the emotional world of the play, and is the source of both insanity and vicious, vindictive cruelty. His Cordelia remains the supreme master-mistress of her own passion:

> *Kent.* O then it moved her.
> *Gent.* Not to a rage, patience and sorow streme,
> Who should expresse her goodliest you have seene,
> Sunshine and raine at once, her smiles and teares,
> Were like a better way those happie smilets,
> That playd on her ripe lip seeme not to know,
> What guests were in her eyes which parted thence,
> As pearles from diamonds dropt in briefe,
> Sorrow would be a raritie most beloved,
> If all could so become it.
>
> (pp. 130–1)

Those proper feminine and filial feelings are figured by natural metaphors of flowing water, beginning with Cordelia's spring of weeping ('an ample teare trild downe'), modulating through the 'streme' , the 'sun shine and raine' of merging patience and sorrow, and moving to a formal sacralisation of this liquid diction in 'holy water'. The Gentleman's idealising emblematization permits Kent overtly to declare that absolute distinctiveness of virtue and vice that is structurally constitutive of the radiant world of romance:

> *Kent.* It is the stars, the stars above us governe our conditions,
> Else one selfe mate and make could not beget,
> Such different issues . . .
>
> (p. 131)

Kent and the Gentleman are here enacting, in anticipation of some significant currents of modern criticism, that project of idealising Cordelia's presence in the play to the point where she is poised to perform the role of a saintly redeemer. The 'reporting' technique of the scene specifically permits that focus on the production of reality in language, as other interpreters reproduce Cordelia in their own preferred form. The text, of course, delivers a different Cordelia, one in whom the emotional tension between daughterly compassion and indignant anger is paralleled by the tension within her cause, between the potentially violent subversiveness of invasion and usurpation, and the proper observation of filial duty. Though modern critics have sought to martyr Cordelia on the altar of female virtues, making of her a pattern of patience and obedience, within the Quarto text there remain strong traces of that 'woman of manlie courage', the Cordelia of historical romance.

As this scene appears only in the Quarto, the standard revisionist method of comparative analysis has been unavailable to scholars, and the textual differentiation therefore relatively uncontroversial. Whatever of Cordelia is represented and produced in this scene, whether that be the saintly female martyr or the empowered romance heroine, is by definition not to be found in the Folio. As Grace Ioppolo says,

> 4.3 does not merely serve to 'emblematize' Cordelia but deliberately and majestically extends the direction of her character which the Quarto has been building for four acts. She is represented as the strong queen and the loving daughter, and her roles merge as she acquires the power to act as one of the play's moral spokespersons . . . Because the Folio lacks these lines . . . it weakens the establishment of moral strength in Cordelia by reducing her at this point in the play to a supporting character rather than a fundamental one.[58]

The 'emblematized' and idealised image of Cordelia is precisely what our dominant critical traditions require. Purged by idealisation of the potent and dangerous associations of otherness (foreignness, manliness, militarism) that collect about her in the Quarto, Cordelia's saintly virtue is ready to withstand the otherwise terminal obstacles of military defeat, capture and execution, as her redemptive and sacrificial virtues are split off into a hypostasised metaphysical realm of indissoluble purity. This is certainly what is done to her in the speeches of Kent and the Gentleman. It is attempted again by

Lear himself, as the defeated contenders are led off the battlefield; though the warrior courage of Cordelia's resentment and indignation breaks through the strategies of idealisation within which patriarchy attempts to confine her:

> (incurd
> *Cor.* We are not the first who with best meaning have
> The worst, for thee oppressed King am I cast downe,
> My selfe could else outfrowne false Fortunes frowne,
> Shall we not see these daughters, and these sisters?
>   *Lear:* No, no, come lets away to prison . . .
> Upon such sacrifices, my *Cordelia*,
> The Gods themselves throw incense . . .
>
> (p. 146)

And it is done to Cordelia again, over and over, in those acts of critical interpretation that seek to replicate the patriarchal idealisation of the Quarto's Gentleman. Indeed if, to entertain for a time the conjecture of revision, the Quarto text *was* edited into the Folio, then this strategy of idealisation must have been a key ideological imperative motivating the revision. It is certainly the case that those famous words so often read as sure and certain hope of the resurrection – 'Looke on her? Looke her lips,/Looke there, looke there' – appear only in the Folio.

Above all, this scene is the strongest link to the old romance narrative from which the Shakespearean tragedies derive. With the scene intact, we have a play in which the discrepancy between traditional happy ending and modern tragedy is stretched to a painful tension, as the dramatic action seems to be moving literally in two quite opposite directions. With Lear's insanity, the torturing of Gloucester, Edmund's success, the text rushes towards the supremacy of disaster. With Cordelia's return, the arrival of allied troops, the continuing determined passive resistance of Kent and Edgar, it turns away towards the once familiar happy ending of restorative romance. In the Folio version, of course, that tension is necessarily reduced by the absence of this particular scene. In the Quarto it remains obstinately in place, disrupting generic uniformity and consistency of tone. It has even been suggested that this element of the play must to its first audiences have raised expectations that the drama would play out towards the familiar happy ending: an expectation that must have terminated in a most bitter and cruel disappointment. Certainly for modern readers, as John Turner puts it, 'the play (unlike any other Shakespearean tragedy) leads us, even when we know it well, to ache after that happy ending implicit in its ancient story-lines'.[59]

X

Where this scene has no Folio counterpart to invite comparison, the mad 'mock-trial' that is peculiar to the Quarto (and that appears in the midst of the scene numbered in the Folio and in modern editions as 3.6) has been the victim of a revisionist argument inflected towards a preference for the imputedly authorial 'cuts' introduced into the Folio version. Although the mock-trial has for centuries been a familiar element in those conflated *King Lear* editions that allow nothing from either text to be lost, revisionists such as Roger Warren and Gary Taylor argue that the Folio text is better without it.

Warren's argument[60] is that the essential action of the 'mock-trial' actually occurs twice, in different forms, in the Quarto text: first in the formal mock-trial of Gonorill and Ragan in the hovel-scene, and again in the encounter between Lear and the blinded Gloster in the scene numbered in the Folio and in modern editions as 4.6. The latter moment involves only three characters, Lear, Gloster and Edgar; and its main substance consists of a dialogue between Lear and Gloster, with Edgar as a silent witness, in which the king offers a corrosive satire on the inadequacy of official justice as a measure of the universal guilt of society and human nature:

> *Glos.* The tricke of that voyce I doe well remember, ist not the King?
> *Lear.* I ever inch a King when I do stare, see how the subject quakes, I pardon that mans life, what was thy cause, adultery? thou shalt not die for adulterie, no the wren goes toot, and the small guilded flie doe letcher in my sight, let copulation thrive, for *Glosters* bastard son was kinder to his father than my daughters got tweene the lawfull sheets . . . see how yon Justice railes upon yon simple theefe, harke in thy eare, handy, dandy, which is the theefe, which is the Justice, thou hast seene a farmers dogge barke at a beggear . . .
> ~And the creature runne from the cur, there thou mightst behold

the great image of authoritie, a dogge, so bade in office, thou rascall
beadle hold thy bloudy hand, why dost thou lash that whore, strip
thine owne backe, thy bloud hotly lusts to use her in that kind for
which thou whipst her, the usurer hangs the cosioner, through tottered
raggs, smal vices do appeare, robes and furd-gownes hides all . . .

(pp. 136–8)

The earlier mock-trial scene, similarly concerned with justice, is
dramatically much more elaborate than this simple exchange. It
involves, as the Quarto stage direction indicates, *Gloster and Lear,
Kent Foole and Tom.* The characters collectively operate as what
Roger Warren calls 'an ensemble of madness', with Lear, the Fool
and Edgar each developing his own particular line in perverse or
insane fantasy:

> *Edg.* *Fretereto* cals me, and tels me *Nero* is an angler in the lake of
> darknes, pray innocent beware the foule fiend.
> *Foole.* Prithe Nunckle tell me, whether a mad man be a Gentle-
> man or a Yeoman.
> *Lear.* A King, a King, to have a thousand with red burning spits
> come hiszing in upon them . . .

(pp. 119–20)

Out of this collaborative lunacy Lear constructs the fantasy of a
formal judicial process in which the absent Gonorill and Ragan are
arraigned for trial. The trial involves the participation of all the
other players, each of whom is cast by Lear in a particular role:

> *Lear.* Ile see their triall first, bring in their evidence, thou
> robbed man of Justice take thy place, & thou his yokefellow
> of equity, bench by his side, you are ot'h commission, sit you too

(p. 120)

The effect is to improvise an absurd parody of formal justice, with
a judicial bench consisting of fools and madmen; charges of absurd
banality ('Arraigne her first tis *Gonoril,* I here take my oath before
this honorable assembly kickt the poore king her father'); and the
role of an absent defendant played by a stool. As such the 'mock-
trial' clearly forms part of that excoriating interrogation of official
justice and political authority for which the plays are justly famous.
In a kingdom where authority is blind and corrupt, and where
power can be freely given to those prepared to override the law, the

subversive perspectives of the insane and dispossessed are more likely to deliver a sense of true justice than the formal powers of state. The transparent innocence of the judgements delivered here – that Gonorill kicked her father, and that Ragan's wickedness is overtly proclaimed by her 'warped lookes' – belongs to a child-like, fairy-tale world where good and evil are distinct and manifest, injuries direct and openly vindictive, and suffering acute and transparently honest. The simple morality of folk-tale, and the elaborate theatrical complexity of saturnalian comedy, unite here to express a genuine popular wisdom.[61]

Roger Warren argues that this earlier scene was probably cut in revision because it presented problems in performance, and because the later exchange between Lear and Gloster does the same job much more effectively.

> . . . in rehearsal or performance it became clear that the focus of the scene had shifted from Lear's mock-justice to eccentric individual detail . . . leading to a generalised sense of chaos. Certainly the effect in performance more often than not seems to amount to no more than the eccentric tricks of a stage full of madmen . . .[62]

It is precisely the collective, 'ensemble' character of the mock-trial that seems to Warren to present problems; and it is exactly those problems that appear to have been resolved by a reviser's preference for the more individual and psychological focus evident in the later scene's parallel satire on justice:

> The big difference between the technique of 3.6 and 4.6 is that the mock trial presents an arraignment of the daughters and of false justice in terms of an ensemble of madness, whereas 4.6 does so by concentrating on Lear's mad mind alone. This scene provides the most effective presentation of the way his mind works, of the logical connections which underlie the mad remarks and which make the speeches effective in both dramatic and psychological terms. These connections help to provide a concentration, a focus, upon the mad remarks which the eccentric digressions of the mock trial tend to dissipate . . .[63]

The particular critical judgement of the mock-trial offered by Warren is therefore consistent with the fundamental argument of revision theory as applied to the Lear-plays, which consists in a general preference for the Folio text, as the 'revised' version, over the unreconstructed, perhaps untested, certainly more experimental textual form to be found in the Quarto:

> . . . whereas the elaborate technique of 3.6 'opens out' Lear's vision of mock justice to involve other kinds of 'madness', 4.6 by contrast *narrows* the focus to the underlying logic of Lear's own extended speeches, and to the very intimate dramatic situation . . . So it seems to me that this very powerful scene expresses in a much more successful manner the 'mad' insights of the mock trial. Perhaps Shakespeare originally intended the trial's treatment of mock justice to pave the way for the later scene, but then the experience of rehearsal or performance made him change his mind.[64]

The value of Warren's comparative analysis lies in its competent characterisation of the textual differences. Much more questionable is his explicit preference for the Folio text, judged superior at the expense of the Quarto. The implicit critical judgement is underpinned by an instinctive preference for a more naturalistic mode of dramatic writing that is clearly at odds with most contemporary assumptions about the early modern theatre. In the Folio text Warren finds some of the structural integrity, stylistic consistency and psychological verisimilitude of the naturalistic 'well-made play': a dramatic action that is 'not only shorter but sharper, more urgent and rapid' (p. 48), a tighter and more coherent 'dramatic structure' (p. 49), and a concentration on the inner movements of the individual mind which is 'effective in both dramatic and psychological terms' (p. 50). What he finds unsatisfactory, chaotic and potentially confusing is that inventive deployment of exactly those theatrical techniques we think of as proper to the early modern public playhouse: ensemble 'company' acting; metadramatic self-reflexivity; fantastic improvisation of meagre theatrical resources; and the subversive carnival energies of a vigorous and sceptical popular culture.

In the same volume Gary Taylor[65] offers a parallel argument about the mock-trial. Taylor adopts an intensely literal approach to the trial itself, which he argues cannot be satirical because the protagonists are not what they momentarily seem: 'The plaintiff is a king; the madman not mad but the sane, good, legitimate son of a nobleman, who will eventually become the champion of justice; the Fool no simple fool . . .'.[66] The mock-trial is not therefore dangerously satirical, and casts 'no aspersions on legal dignity'.[67] If the scene does not then attain the stylistic and satirical coherence bestowed on it by the imposed structure of Lear's fantasy, its contents are bound to seem merely eccentric, disjointed, incoherent. Taylor agrees with Warren that the scene is 'chaotic' – 'the scene, to some degree, fails to organize a structure of perceptions that will guide an audience to a recognition of its range of meanings'[68] – and that the Folio's redaction is clearly superior, since it provides 'a perceptible, emotionally and intellectually satisfying structure'.[69]

It is interesting to consider why, given that the primary objective of revisionist criticism of these plays is to establish that both texts were of Shakespearean origin, it should be thought necessary to make such sharp discriminations of *value* between one text and another. If both the hypothesis of revision, and everything that Warren and Taylor say about the stylistic discrepancies between the two texts were accepted, all that is necessarily implied is that there were obvious conflicts of artistic direction within the contingent theatrical culture. Perhaps the distance between Folio and Quarto does represent, in miniature, the movement from a more experimental to a more 'naturalistic' mode of theatrical construction that certainly took place across the period. But these are symptoms of historical process, and do not readily facilitate judgements on a common scale of quality between texts that are fundamentally incommensurable, precisely because culturally diverse.

In fact the revisionists have captured their own procedures in a trap of their own devising. If both texts are to be traced to an origin in Shakespearean authorship, then one must represent second thoughts and changed intentions, which in turn must indicate dissatisfaction with the original formulation. But the traditional stamp of Shakespearean authorship is the quality of its products. How can something be both Shakespearean, and of a quality inferior to something else that is not only equally Shakespearean but in many ways very similar? Gary Taylor discloses a significant embarrassment arising out of this contradiction:

> There is always something disconcerting, for reader and writer alike, in the suggestion that any passage in Shakespeare's mature work in any way or for any reason 'fails', and that the play might be better without it. The mad trial is so good, by the normal standards of this

[51]

world, that perhaps no one but Shakespeare could have been
dissatisfied with it.[70]

The 'normal standards of this world' are pessimistically assumed to
be abysmally low, and whatever is Shakespearean by definition
transcends them. This model posits a type of critical discrimination
that takes place at that supreme level where Shakespeare judged his
own work; a plane of quasi-divine perception far beyond the reach
of mere mortals. If, however, we are prepared to re-think this
problem outside the parameters of revision theory and authorial
intention, together with the arcane metaphysical concepts these
theories seem inevitably to carry with them, it becomes clear that
the critical judgements expressing preference for one text over
another are being made by mere mortals such as Warren and
Taylor, and made on the basis of 'the normal standards of this
world', however depressingly low those may be. René Weis puts
the same case in a more straightforwardly consumerist, less
theological way: 'The fact that neither of the two separate texts
contains everything that Shakespeare wrote need not be taken to
imply that he therefore got it wrong the first time round.'[71] We
should be as satisfied with that which once dissatisfied Shakespeare,
as we are with that which finally met with his satisfaction.

XI

Just as the dominant editorial tradition has been founded on an
attempt to restore by collation, conflation and emendation a
textualisation approximating to a lost 'original', so the dominant
critical tradition addressing the Lear-plays as tragedy has evaluated
them within an interpretative context governed by a search for the
play's moral philosophy. From G. Wilson Knight's view of *King
Lear* as a parable of Christian sacrifice and spiritual regeneration, to
Jan Kott's perception of the play as depicting the ethical vacuity and
moral exhaustion of the modern world,[72] '*King Lear*' has been
expected to deliver some kind of authorially intended and deliberately
composed world-view. In the course of the debate around revision,
the editorial and critical agendas have become interestingly inter-
twined. Since the founding modern critical debate (1930-70)[73]
produced an interpretative spectrum wholly concentrated on the

play's moral philosophy, but ranging widely from 'optimistic' to 'pessimistic' readings, it seemed inevitable that bibliographical comparisons between the 1608 and 1623 texts should also focus on variations within the same interpretative field. Thus the textual debate, with its enforced concentration on the relationship between the two texts, has tended to concern itself with the same problems of interpretation, and tried to assess how each text scores on the same scale of values – is *'King Lear'* an uplifting affirmation of the possibilities of spiritual redemption, or a bleak invocation of an empty universe? Do the gods of the play throw incense on sacrifice, or wantonly kill men and women like flies?

If the obvious variations between the texts are attributed to authorial revision, and both 1608 and 1623 versions contained within the great metacategory of the 'author', then each text can be expected to embody and express a distinct, though clearly iterable, authorial perspective. Revisionist bibliography, in short, needs the outdated critical concept of authorial intention. In general, it is noteworthy that bibliographical studies have tended to remain resistant to new currents of critical theory and practice. In the case of *'King Lear'*, the critical–bibliographical debate has tended to revolve around Bradleian character-study, a pseudo-Aristotelean conception of tragedy as an immanent aesthetic form, and the quasi-religious, moralistic criticism associated particularly with G. Wilson Knight.

The focus on 'character' seems to reflect an extreme critical conservatism, but has been justified by the argument that textual variations (usually involving the addition, subtraction and differential allocation of 'lines') affect characterisation more obviously than other aesthetic categories. Gary Taylor thus observes of the 'two-text debate', that 'much of the argument has involved alleged differences in the presentation of character. Character criticism is, of course, intellectually unfashionable at the moment, but studies of pervasive imagery and themes could hardly be expected to differentiate two strata of composition.'[74] The tools of criticism are, then, in Taylor's terms, 'character', 'imagery' and 'themes'. Only the first of these, albeit currently 'unfashionable', can be said to reflect the influence of textual variation.

The interaction within the *'King Lear'* two-text debate of

Introduction

Bradleian character-criticism and Wilson Knight moralism can be demonstrated from a series of discussions addressing the variations or alterations in the textual presentation of Albany and Edgar, and their influence on each text's conclusion. The final speech of the play, though common to both texts, is spoken by Albany in Q and by Edgar in F. The debate was initiated by Michael Warren in a 1978 paper on 'Quarto and Folio *King Lear* and the Interpretation of Albany and Edgar'.[75] Gary Taylor pursued this line in *The Division of the Kingdoms*, his comparative discussion of the roles of Albany and Edgar framed within the same assumptions about tragedy as an ethical discourse, and focusing particularly on the dramatic conclusion of each text: 'To Michael Warren's admirable account of the Folio's magnification of Edgar, largely at Albany's expense, I have nothing to add; but neither he nor Urkowitz remarks on the fact that Edgar fills the role of chief moral survivor much more comfortably than either Albany or Kent.'[76] It is axiomatic to this argument that tragedy ends with a recomposition of social order and a re-establishment of moral integrity, directed or presided over by a key 'moral survivor'. Edgar seems to Taylor to fill that role admirably: he is 'a representative of moral continuity',[77] whose strengthened role in the Folio 'naturally therefore strengthens the promise of moral continuity after the tragedy . . . Some sense of hope, transcendence, spiritual consolation, the Folio ending . . . offers us'.[78]

René Weis follows loyally in this tradition, arguing that the role of Albany is substantially weakened, and Edgar's substantially strengthened, between Q and F. Her particular evidence for Albany's progressive enervation is the absence from F of some speeches (this text, pp. 128–9) in which he stands up to his wife, an exhibition of manliness and personal probity considered indispensable to the holding of public office: 'Albany needs to sever himself from Gonoril and a married life with her. If he is to bear the standard of decency and duty in the play and lead his people, he must spell out his rejection of Gonoril's evil and his past married life with her'.[79] The relative strengthening of Edgar's role indicates 'a wider conceptual transformation', in the course of which the revising Shakespeare shifted the ultimate conferral of moral power from the legitimate but poorly qualified heir, Albany, to the figure

Introduction

who claims power by right of suffering and moral growth. By virtue of 'the fact that Albany speaks the last lines in Q and Edgar in F . . . F would appear to play down the importance of Albany: after all, the concluding lines are very important here where the speaker assumes the mantle of the ultimate moral authority in the play'.[80] The attribution of that status to Edgar is described by Weis as 'a radical and aesthetically conscious act', aligning power with virtue, and allowing the meek to inherit the earth.

A number of shared presuppositions derived from a conservative critical agenda have here very clearly obstructed critical reading. It should surely be apparent that both texts, though in F much more decisively than in Q, defy and defeat any expectation of restoration, recomposition or 'moral continuity'. In Q Albany offers the kingdom to Edgar and Kent as joint rulers:

> *Duke*: Beare them from hence, our present busines
> Is to generall woe, friends of my soule, you twaine
> Rule in this kingdome, and the goard state sustaine.
>
> (p. 155)

As the sole surviving member of the aristocracy to whom Lear granted the divided kingdom, Albany should constitutionally inherit: but he appears not to want the job. There is already therefore a distinct sense, inconceivable in a historical drama but possible in a romance (and I would add, in a Shakespearean tragedy), that there is no recomposition: that monarchy itself has died with Lear, and that the kingdom exhibits a condition of what John Turner has called 'terminal collapse': 'We are left at the end not with dogma but with dead loss.'[81]

Kent certainly declines the offer: his allegiance is to a lost world-order, an absolute attachment to 'a civilization lost with anguish for all time'.[82] In the present text, Albany's summing-up speech is not at all what might be expected from an agent of social reconstruction, but it does at least express some sense of human solidarity among the younger and surviving generation, symbolised by himself and Edgar. Kent, together with Lear and Gloster, belongs to a superseded generation, which vanishes together with the world it governed. Albany and Edgar remain to pick up the pieces. Albany's final speech is not, however, a formal declaration of

[55]

reconstruction, the kingdom 'under new management', but an elegiac reflection on the incommensurability of that old lost world and what survives. Abandoning his formal attempt to restore order, Albany asserts that such political language is beside the point, and only the language of feeling remains valid. Edgar, in this version, says absolutely nothing (even less than Cordelia). His eloquent silence is a suitable testament to the sovereignty of emotion, but distinctly unpromising in a figurehead of government.

More decisively still does F insist on the finality of the kingdom's terminal collapse. Albany again offers the job of ruler to the only two available candidates: but this time both appear to decline. It seems to have escaped the notice of revisionist critics that in F, Edgar seems no more inclined to accept sovereign responsibility than is Kent. It is very clear that in both texts the language required by the situation, 'what we ought to say', is identified as that formal language of political recomposition that the survivors find so embarrassingly inappropriate. The language of feeling, that transparent language Lear had discovered in his reconciliation with Cordelia, necessarily has the ultimate effect of deferring the moment of political restitution (just as Lear and Cordelia in the 'recognition' scene – he speaking the new dialect of sincerity, she adhering to the traditional rhetoric of power – do not really recognise one another at all, since they fail even to speak a common language). Edgar's elegiac tribute to the authorities of Lear's vanished world co-exists with a humble and despairing expression of inadequacy. This is not what we have been taught by our critical traditions to expect from the final resolution of a 'Shakespearean tragedy'.

XII

Clearly the two *King Lear*-plays acknowledged as 'Shakespearean' are more closely linked to one another than they are to the other extant Lear-narratives: both share the same tragic structure, and both differ equally from those versions that retain the historical and romance 'happy ending', where tragedy is deferred and naturalised by the chronicle method (where the deaths of Lear and Cordelia are

Introduction

not part of a single tragic action, but the outcome of a longer historical process, literally another story), and by the healing and irenic potencies of romance. None the less, it can be demonstrated that both versions are remarkably open to generic influences, and that those influences operate unevenly across the two versions. I have resisted the temptation to argue that the two texts can be discriminated in some absolute sense: that one is, for example, consistently more tragic, or more consistently romantic, than the other. It can be shown, however, that within each text, always locally, and occasionally (as in the distinctive Quarto scene descriptive of Cordelia's return from France) structurally, different generic influences are interacting to produce a certain textual volatility that is at odds with our assumption of a clear and absolute 'tragic structure'.

The textual destabilisation of contemporary bibliography thus opens up further possibilities for an interpretative deconstruction of the 'Lear'-texts in terms of their openness to the manifold generic possibilities active in the collective body of Lear-narratives. This project requires a rapprochement of cutting-edge bibliography and up-to-date critical theory. Above all, it requires the general availability of an edition of the original Quarto text, freed from both its traditional attachment to the Folio, and from the distorting interference of modern editors. *Shakespearean Originals* here offers such an edition, not as the final word on modern presentations of the text, but only as a positive editorial and theoretical contribution to an already vigorous and developing debate.

NOTES AND REFERENCES

1. Stanley Wells and Gary Taylor, with John Jowett and William Montgomery (eds), 'The History of King Lear', in *William Shakespeare: The Complete Works* (Oxford: Oxford University Press, 1986); Michael Warren (ed.), *The Complete 'King Lear' 1608–1623* (Berkeley: University of California Press, 1989); René Weis (ed.), *'King Lear': A Parallel-Text Edition* (London: Longman, 1993); and Jay L. Halio (ed.), *The First Quarto of King Lear* (Cambridge: Cambridge University Press, 1994). Weis and Halio both use the title coined by Wells and Taylor, *The History of King Lear*. The full title of the 1608 publication was *M. William Shak-speare: his true chronicle historie of the life and*

death of King Lear and his three daughters. With the unfortunate life of Edgar, sonne and heire to the earle of Gloster, and his fullen and assumed humor of Tom of Bedlam.

2. See Kenneth Muir (ed.), *King Lear* (London: Methuen, 1952); and G.K. Hunter (ed.), *King Lear* (Harmondsworth: Penguin, 1972). The revised Arden editions will evidently draw attention to the differential provenance of texts by using different typefaces: e.g. Jonathan Bate's edition of '*Titus Andronicus*', to be published in March 1995, is based on the First Quarto, *The Most Lamentable Romaine Tragedie of Titus Andronicus* (1594), but interpolates one scene (modern editions 3.2) that appears only in the Folio version, *The Tragedie of Titus Andronicus* (1623). The conflated scene is apparently to be typographically discriminated from its Quarto context. I am grateful to Ann Thompson, joint general editor of the revised Arden series, for this information, and to Routledge for an advance copy of Bate's introduction to his edition of *The Most Lamentable Romaine Tragedie of Titus Andronicus*.

3. Muir (ed.), *King Lear* (Arden Shakespeare), p. xvi.

4. A.W. Pollard, *Shakespeare Folios and Quartos* (London: Methuen, 1909), p. 76; and *Shakespeare's Fight with the Pirates*, 2nd edn (Cambridge: Cambridge University Press, 1920), pp. 50–1.

5. W.W. Greg, 'The Function of Bibliography in Literary Criticism Illustrated in a Study of the Text of *King Lear*', in J. C. Maxwell (ed.), *The Collected Papers of Sir Walter W. Greg* (Oxford: Clarendon Press, 1966), p. 287.

6. G.I. Duthie, *Elizabethan Shorthand and the First Quarto of King Lear* (Oxford: Blackwell, 1949).

7. Although the memorial reconstruction theory has, according to Jay L. Halio, 'few, if any, advocates', it can in recent practice be found vigorously and aggressively defended. Inveterate champions include Brian Vickers, who claims that the studies of Duthie and Alfred Hart 'irrefutably confirmed' the view that 'the pirated texts were the work of actors who had probably performed in the plays . . . and put the text together from memory'; and Harold Jenkins: 'I am aware that theories of memorial reconstruction have sometimes come under attack in recent years. But . . . such a process . . . offers a wholly convincing explanation.' See *Times Literary Supplement*, 24 December 1993, pp. 5–6, and 15 April 1994, p. 17.

8. Alice Walker, *Textual Problems of the First Folio* (Cambridge: Cambridge University Press, 1953).

9. G.I. Duthie (ed.), *King Lear* (1949). Duthie subsequently abandoned this view in favour of Walker's theory.

10. MacDonald P. Jackson has, for instance, observed that both memorial reconstruction and literary revision would actually produce exactly the same kinds of evidence: 'The wellnigh universal tendency of revising authors to vary phrases that are exactly repeated in an early version of their work, to shift words, phrases, lines and longer passages from one part of their poem, story or play to another, to emphasize by repetition certain key words and images . . . inevitably creates apparent evidence in the original text of anticipation, recollection, transposition . . . – all the traditional stigmata of a memorial report.' See Jackson's 'Fluctuating Variation – Author, Annotator or Actor?', in Gary Taylor and Michael Warren (eds), *The Division of the Kingdoms: Shakespeare's Two Versions of 'King Lear'* (Oxford: Clarendon Press, 1983), p. 331.

11. Steven Urkowitz, *Shakespeare's Revision of 'King Lear'* (Princeton: Princeton University Press, 1980).

12. Peter Blayney, *The Texts of 'King Lear' and their Origins* (Cambridge, 1982).

13. *The Division of the Kingdoms* featured, among others, essays by key revisionists Stanley Wells, Steven Urkowitz, Michael Warren, Paul Werstine and Gary Taylor.

14. The Oxford *Complete Works* was published in two forms, a modernised text, and an 'old-spelling' version that still entailed, paradoxically, a high level of editorial interference. See Stanley Wells and Gary Taylor, with John Jowett and William Montgomery (eds), *William Shakespeare: The Complete Works, Original-spelling Edition* (Oxford: Oxford University Press, 1986); and for a critique of the latter's editorial policy, see Graham Holderness and Bryan Loughrey, 'Text and Stage: Shakespeare, Bibliography and Performance Studies', *New Theatre Quarterly*, vol. IX (May 1993), pp. 179–91.

15. Stanley Wells, 'Theatricalizing Shakespeare's Texts', in *New Theatre Quarterly*, vol. VII (May 1991), p. 186.

16. David Bevington, 'Determining the Indeterminate: The Oxford Shakespeare', *Shakespeare Quarterly*, vol. 20 (1968–70), pp. 501, 502.

17. Margreta de Grazia and Peter Stallybrass, 'The Materiality of the Shakespearean Text', in *Shakespeare Quarterly*, vol. 44 (1993), pp. 255–83.

18. *Ibid.*, p. 279.

19. The revisionist position is set out concisely on pp. xxxiv–xxv of the 'General Introduction' to the Oxford *Complete Works*. The theory of the 'directorial para-text' is expounded in Stanley Wells and Gary Taylor, with John Jowett and William Montgomery, *William Shakespeare: A Textual Companion* (Oxford: Clarendon, 1987), p. 2.

20. Wells, 'Theatricalizing Shakespeare's Texts', p. 185.

21. I use this phrase advisedly. The 'onlie begetter' of the *Sonnets* was not, of course, the author.

22. Wells *et al.*, *Textual Companion*, p. 69. A similar metaphor is used to characterise the role of the editor in relation to the author: 'The authority of scholars derives from their capacity or their claim to recover and interpret the revered texts of . . . cultural "fathers"; like priests, they tell us what the father meant; by doing so, they earn the affection of their "mother" (the Church; or its secular equivalent, the university)', p. 7.

23. Warren's project is discussed at length in de Grazia and Stallybrass, 'The Materiality of the Shakespearean Text'; and in Graham Holderness, Bryan Loughrey and Andrew Murphy, ' "What's the Matter?" Shakespeare and Textual Theory', *Textual Practice* (forthcoming, Spring 1995).

24. De Grazia and Stallybrass, 'The Materiality of the Shakespearean Text', p. 255.

25. *Ibid.*, p. 261.

26. *Ibid.*, p. 283.

27. Paul Werstine, review of Warren's *The Complete 'King Lear'*, in *Shakespeare Quarterly*, vol. 44 (Summer 1993), pp. 236–7.

28. Michel Foucault, 'What is an Author?', in Paul Rabinow (ed.), *The Foucault Reader* (New York: Pantheon, 1984), p. 119.

29. René Weis (ed.), *'King Lear': A Parallel-Text Edition* (London: Longman, 1993), p. 5.

30. *Ibid.*

31. Jay L. Halio (ed.), *The First Quarto of 'King Lear'* (Cambridge: Cambridge University Press, 1994), p. v.

32. *Ibid.*, p. ix.

33. *Ibid.*, p. vi.

34. Gibbons's assertion, in a text published in mid-1994, that 'these texts are not readily available' is particularly remarkable in its occlusion of *Shakespearean Originals*, which began to publish editions in July 1992, and has already issued the 1600 Quarto of 'Henry V': see Graham Holderness and Bryan Loughrey (eds), *The Chronicle History of Henry the fift, With his battell fought at* Agin Court *in* France. *Togither with* Auntient Pistoll (Hemel Hempstead: Harvester Wheatsheaf, 1993).

35. Quoted here from Kenneth Muir's Arden edition of *King Lear*, V.iii.323–6, which follows the 1623 text from *Mr William Shakespeares Comedies, Histories, & Tragedies*:

> *Edg.* The waight of this sad time we must obey,
> Speake what we feele, not what we ought to say:

Introduction

The oldest hath borne most, we that are yong,
Shall never see so much, nor liue so long.

36. Nahum Tate, in James Black (ed.), *The History of King Lear* (Lincoln: University of Nebraska Press, 1975), p. 95.
37. Nahum Tate, 'Dedicatory Letter' to *The History of King Lear*, see Black (ed.), p. 2.
38. Maynard Mack, from *King Lear in Our Time* (1969), quoted from Frank Kermode (ed.) *Shakespeare: King Lear, A Casebook* (London: Macmillan, 1969), p. 55.
39. From Raphael Holinshed's *Chronicles of England, Scotland and Ireland* (1587), vol. 2, quoted from Muir (ed.), *King Lear*, p. 236.
40. *The Faerie Queene*, Book Two, Canto X, stanzas 31–2; J.C. Smith and E. De Selincourt (eds), *The Poetical Works of Edmund Spenser* (Oxford: Oxford University Press, 1912), p. 121.
41. Holinshed, quoted from Muir (ed.) *King Lear*, p. 234.
42. John Higgins, *The Mirror for Magistrates* (1574), quoted from Muir (ed.), *King Lear*, p. 239.
43. *M. William Shak-speare: his true chronicle historie of the life and death of King Lear and his three daughters*, this edition, p. 71.
44. Holinshed, quoted from Muir (ed.), *King Lear*, p. 237.
45. Spenser, *The Faerie Queene*, Book Two, Canto X, stanza 32; Smith and De Selincourt (eds), *Poetical Works*, p. 121.
46. Muir (ed.), *King Lear*, p. xxxvii.
47. J.F. Danby, *Shakespeare's Doctrine of Nature: A Study of 'King Lear'* (London: Faber, 1961).
48. John Turner discusses the significance of such 'mythical charters' to the *King Lear*-plays in Graham Holderness, Nick Potter and John Turner, *Shakespeare: The Play of History* (London: Macmillan, 1987), pp. 91–4.
49. See G. Wilson Knight, *The Wheel of Fire: Interpretations of Shakespearean Tragedy* (London: Chattos and Windus, 1930).
50. From *The Tragedie of King Lear*, in *Mr William Shakespeares Comedies, Histories, & Tragedies* (1623). Quoted from Charlton Hinman (ed.), *The Norton Facsimile: The First Folio of Shakespeare*, (New York: W.W. Norton, 1968), p. 804.
51. W.W. Greg, 'Time, Place and Politics in *King Lear*', in J.C. Maxwell (ed.), *The Collected Papers of Sir Walter W. Greg*; and M. Doran, *The Text of King Lear* (Stanford, 1931).
52. Gary Taylor, 'Monopolies, Show Trials, Disaster, and Invasion: King Lear and Censorship', in Taylor and Warren (eds), *The Division of the Kingdoms*, p. 80.

53. Weis, *King Lear: A Parallel-Text Edition*, p. 31.
54. Greg, 'Time, Place and Politics in *King Lear*'.
55. See Taylor, 'Monopolies, Show Trials, Disaster, and Invasion: *King Lear* and Censorship', p. 80.
56. De Grazia and Stallybrass, 'The Materiality of the Shakespearean Text', p. 279.
57. Grace Ioppolo, *Revising Shakespeare* (Cambridge, Mass.: Harvard University Press, 1991), focuses particularly on the differential representations of Cordelia as heroine between the two textualisations.
58. *Ibid.*, p. 171.
59. Turner, in Holderness, Potter and Turner, *Shakespeare: The Play of History*, p. 95.
60. Roger Warren, 'The Folio Omission of the the Mock Trial: Motives and Consequences', in Taylor and Warren (eds), *The Division of the Kingdoms*, pp. 45–57.
61. This can clearly be related to those plebianising tendencies of the Quartos noted by Leah Marcus in 'Levelling Shakespeare: Local Customs and Local Texts', *Shakespeare Quarterly*, vol. 42, no. 2 (1991), pp. 168–78.
62. Warren, 'The Folio Omission of the Mock Trial', p. 47.
63. *Ibid.*, p. 50.
64. *Ibid.*, pp. 52–3.
65. See Taylor, 'Monopolies, Show Trials, Disaster, and Invasion: *King Lear* and Censorship', pp. 88–101.
66. *Ibid.*, p. 89.
67. *Ibid.*
68. *Ibid.*, p. 92.
69. *Ibid.*, p. 100.
70. *Ibid.*, p. 101.
71. Weis, '*King Lear*': A Parallel-Text Edition, p. 1.
72. Knight, *The Wheel of Fire*, and Jan Kott, *Shakespeare our Contemporary* 1965.
73. Frank Kermode (ed.), *Shakespeare: King Lear, A Casebook* (London: Macmillan, 1969), provides a useful anthology of views across this period, its parameters marked by contributions from Knight (1930) and Kott (1967).
74. Gary Taylor, '*King Lear*: The Date and Authorship of the Folio Version', in Taylor and Warren (eds), *The Division of the Kingdoms*, p. 422.
75. Michael Warren, 'Quarto and Folio *King Lear* and the Interpretation of Albany and Edgar', in David Bevington and Jay L. Halio (eds),

Shakespeare: Pattern of Excelling Nature (Newark: University of Delaware Press, 1978), pp. 95–117.

76. Gary Taylor, '*King Lear*: the Date and Authorship of the Folio Version', in Taylor and Warren (eds), *The Division of the Kingdoms*, p. 425.

77. *Ibid.*, p. 425.

78. *Ibid.*, p. 427.

79. Weis, '*King Lear*': *A Parallel-Text Edition*, p. 1.

80. *Ibid.*, pp. 7–8.

81. John Turner, in Holderness, Potter and Turner, *Shakespeare: The Play of History*, p. 97.

82. *Ibid.*

Select Bibliography

Blayney, Peter, *The Texts of 'King Lear' and their Origins* (Cambridge: Cambridge University Press, 1982).

Cloud, Random (Randall McLeod), 'The Marriage of Good and Bad Quartos', *Shakespeare Quarterly*, vol. 33 (1982).

Danby, J.F., *Shakespeare's Doctrine of Nature: A Study of 'King Lear'* (London: Faber, 1961).

Duthie, G.I., *Elizabethan Shorthand and the First Quarto of King Lear* (Oxford: Blackwell, 1984).

Goldberg, Jonathan, 'Textual Properties', *Shakespeare Quarterly*, vol. 37 (1986).

Grazia, Margreta de, *Shakespeare Verbatim* (Oxford: Oxford University Press, 1991).

Grazia, Margreta de and Peter Stallybrass, 'The Materiality of the Shakespearean Text', *Shakespeare Quarterly*, vol. 44 (Fall 1993).

Greg, W.W., 'The Function of Bibliography in Literary Criticism Illustrated in a Study of the Text of *King Lear*', in J. C. Maxwell (ed.), *The Collected Papers of Sir Walter W. Greg* (Oxford: Clarendon Press, 1966).

Halio, Jay (ed.), *The First Quarto of 'King Lear'* (Cambridge: Cambridge University Press, 1994).

Hinman, Charlton (ed.), *The Norton Facsimile: The First Folio of Shakespeare* (New York: W.W. Norton, 1968).

Holderness, Graham and Bryan Loughrey, 'Text and Stage: Shakespeare, Bibliography and Performance Studies', *New Theatre Quarterly*, vol. IX, no. 34 (May 1993).

Holderness, Graham, Bryan Loughrey and Andrew Murphy, ' "What's the Matter?" Shakespeare and Textual Theory', *Textual Practice* (forthcoming, Spring 1995).

Holderness, Graham, Nick Potter and John Turner, *Shakespeare: The Play of History* (London: Macmillan, 1987).

Hunter, G.K. (ed.), *King Lear* (Harmondsworth: Penguin, 1972).

Select Bibliography

Iopollo, Grace, *Revising Shakespeare* (Cambridge, Mass.: Harvard University Press, 1991).

Kermode, Frank (ed.), *Shakespeare: King Lear, A Casebook* (London: Macmillan, 1969).

Knight, G. Wilson, *The Wheel of Fire: Interpretations of Shakespearean Tragedy* (London: Chatto & Windus, 1930).

Muir, Kenneth (ed.), *King Lear* (London: Methuen, 1952).

Pollard, A.W., *Shakespeare's Fight with the Pirates*, 2nd edn (Cambridge: Cambridge University Press, 1920).

Tate, Nahum, *The History of King Lear*, edited by James Black (Lincoln: University of Nebraska Press, 1975).

Urkowitz, Steven, *Shakespeare's Revision of 'King Lear'* (Princeton: Princeton University Press, 1980).

Warren, Michael, 'Quarto and Folio *King Lear* and the Interpretation of Albany and Edgar', in David Bevington and Jay L. Halio (eds), *Shakespeare: Pattern of Excelling Nature* (Newark: University of Delaware Press, 1978).

Warren, Michael (ed.), *The Complete 'King Lear' 1608–1623* (Berkeley: University of California Press, 1989).

Weis, René (ed.), *'King Lear': A Parallel-Text Edition* (London: Longman, 1993).

Wells, Stanley and Gary Taylor, with John Jowett and William Montgomery (eds), *William Shakespeare: The Complete Works* (Oxford: Oxford University Press, 1986).

Wells, Stanley, 'Theatricalizing Shakespeare's Texts', *New Theatre Quarterly*, vol. VII (May 1991).

Textual History

T H E First Quarto '*Lear*' (Q1) was originally published in 1608, by Nicholas Okes for Nathaniel Butter. Some dozen copies survive, most of which differ from one another, to the extent of about 150 readings, as a consequence of the process of 'continuous copy' (i.e. the sheets being altered as they went through the press). A second edition (Q2) was printed in 1619 by Thomas Pavier, as part of his aborted attempt to publish a collection of Shakespeare quartos. An example of Q2, with its false publication date of 1602, can be found bound together with a genuine first edition in the volume 'Malone 35' (Arch. G. d. 42) in the Bodleian Library.

The present text is derived from a copy of Q1 known as the 'Gorehambury Quarto', from its ownership by the Earl of Verulam, which is held on deposit in the Bodleian (Dep. e. 3).

Textual History

The title-page appears as

M. William Shak-speare:

HIS

True Chronicle Historie of the life and
death of King LEAR and his three
Daughters.

With the vnfortunate life of Edgar, *sonne*
and heire to the Earle of Gloster, and his
sullen and assumed humor of
TOM of Bedlam:

As it was played before the Kings Maiestie at Whitehall upon
S. Stephans *night in Christmas Hollidayes.*

By his Maiesties seruants playing vsually at the Gloabe
on the Bancke-side.

LONDON,
Printed for *Nathaniel Butter*, and are to be sold at his shop in *Pauls*
Church-yard at the signe of the Pide Bull neere
St. *Austins* Gate. 1608.

This particular text was published 'collographically' by W.W. Greg in
the *Shakespeare Quarto Facsimile* series (Collographic Art Printers/
T. & A. Constable, 1939), and subsequently reissued in the form of a
lithographic reproduction of the 1939 facsimile sheets (Oxford University Press, 1964), with an additional note by Charlton Hinman.

As indicated in the 'Introduction', the Quarto has been published
in a number of recent modern editions: *The History of King Lear*, in
William Shakespeare: The Complete Works, and *William Shakespeare:
The Complete Works, Original-spelling Edition*, both edited by Stanley
Wells and Gary Taylor, with John Jowett and William Montgomery
(Oxford: Oxford University Press, 1986); *The Complete 'King Lear'
1608–1623*, edited by Michael Warren (Berkeley: University of
California Press, 1989); *King Lear: A Parallel-Text Edition*, edited by
René Weis (London: Longman, 1993); and *The First Quarto of King
Lear*, edited by Jay L. Halio (Cambridge: Cambridge University
Press, 1994).

M. William Shak-speare:

HIS
True Chronicle Historie of the life and
death of King L E A R and his three
Daughters.

With the vnfortunate life of Edgar, *sonne*
and heire to the Earle of Gloster, and his
sullen and assumed humor of
T O M of Bedlam :

As it was played before the Kings Maiestie at Whitehall vpon
S. Stephans night in Christmas Hollidayes.

By his Maiesties seruants playing vsually at the Gloabe
on the Bancke-side.

LONDON,
Printed for *Nathaniel Butter*, and are to be sold at his shop in *Pauls*
Church-yard at the signe of the Pide Bull neero
St. *Austins* Gate. 1 6 0 8.

And

M. William Shak-speare:

HIS

Historie, of King Lear

Enter Kent, Gloster, and Bastard.

Kent.

I Thought the King had more affected the Duke of *Albany*
then *Cornwell.*

Glost. It did allwaies seeme so to us, but now in the
division of the kingdomes, it appeares not which of the
Dukes he values most, for the equalities are so weighed, that
curiositie in neither, can make choise of eithers moytie.

Kent. Is not this your sonne my Lord?

Glost. His breeding sir hath beene at my charge, I have so
often blusht to acknowledge him, that now I am braz'd to it.

Kent. I cannot conceive you.

Glost. Sir, this young fellowes mother Could, wherupon
shee grew round wombed, and had indeed Sir a sonne for her
cradle, ere she had a husband for her bed, doe you smell a
fault?

Kent. I cannot wish the fault undone, the issue of it being
so proper.

Glost. But I have sir a sonne by order of Law, some yeare
elder then this, who yet is no deerer in my account, though
this knave came something sawcely into the world before hee
was sent for, yet was his mother faire, there was good sport

at his makeing & the whoreson must be acknowledged, do
you know this noble gentleman *Edmund*?

Bast. No my Lord.

Glost. My Lord of Kent, remember him hereafter as my
honorable friend..

Bast. My services to your Lordship.

Kent. I must love you, and sue to know you better.

Bast. Sir I shall study deserving.

Glost. Hee hath beene out nine yeares, and away hee shall
againe, the King is comming.

*Sound a Sennet, Enter one bearing a Coronet, then Lear, then the
Dukes of Albany, and Cornwell, next Gonorill, Regan, Cordelia,
with followers.*

Lear. Attend my Lords of France and Burgundy, *Gloster.*

Glost. I shall my Leige.

Lear. Meane time we will expresse our darker purposes,
The map there; know we have divided
In three, our kingdome; and tis our first intent,
To shake all cares and busines of our state,
Confirming them on yonger yeares,
The two great Princes *France* and *Burgundy*,
Great ryvals in our youngest daughters love,
Long in our Court have made their amorous sojourne,
And here are to be answerd, tell me my daughters,
Which of you shall we say doth love us most,
That we our largest bountie may extend,
Where merit doth most challenge it,
Gonorill our eldest borne, speake first?

Gon. Sir I do love you more then words can weild the
Dearer then eye-sight, space or libertie,   (matter,
Beyond what can be valued rich or rare,
No lesse then life; with grace, health, beautie, honour,
As much a child ere loved, or father friend,
A love that makes breath poore, and speech unable,
Beyond all manner of so much I love you.

Cor. What shall *Cordelia* doe, love and be silent.

Lear. Of al these bounds, even from this line to this,
With shady forrests, and wide skirted meades,
We make thee Lady, to thine and *Albaines* issue,
Be this perpetuall, what saies our second daughter?
Our deerest *Regan*, wife to *Cornwell*, speake?

Reg. Sir I am made of the selfe same mettall that my sister is,
And prize me at her worth in my true heart,
I find she names my very deed of love, onely she came short,
That I professe my selfe an enemie to all other joyes,
Which the most precious square of sense possesses,
And I find am alone felicitate, in your deere highnes love.

Cord. Then poore *Cord.* & yet not so, since I am sure
My loves more richer then my tonge.

Lear. To thee and thine hereditarie ever
Remaine this ample third of our faire kingdome,
No lesse in space, validity, and pleasure,
Then that confirm'd on *Gonorill*, but now our joy,
Although the last, not least in our deere love,
What can you say to win a third, more opulent
Then your sisters.

Cord. Nothing my Lord.   (againe.

Lear. How, nothing can come of nothing, speake

Cord. Unhappie that I am, I cannot heave my heart into
my mouth, I love your Majestie according to my bond, nor
more nor lesse.

Lear. Goe to, goe to, mend your speech a little,
Least it may mar your fortunes.

Cord. Good my Lord,
You have begot me, bred me, loved me,
I returne those duties backe as are right fit,
Obey you, love you, and most honour you,
Why have my sisters husbands if they say they love you all,
Happely when I shall wed, that Lord whose hand
Must take my plight, shall cary halfe my love with him,
Halfe my care and duty, sure I shall never
Mary like my sisters, to love my father all.

Lear. But goes this with thy heart?

Cord. I good my Lord.

Lear. So yong and so untender,

Cord. So yong my Lord and true.

Lear. Well let it be so, thy truth then be thy dower,
For by the sacred radience of the Sunne,
The mistresse of *Heccat*, and the might,
By all the operation of the orbs,
From whome we doe exsist and cease to be
Heere I disclaime all my paternal care,
Propinquitie and property of blood,
And as a stranger to my heart and me
Hould thee from this for ever, the barbarous *Scythyan*,
Or he that makes his generation
Messes to gorge his appetite
Shall bee as well neighbour'd, pittyed and relieved
As thou my sometime daughter.

   Kent. Good my Liege   (his wrath,

   Lear. Peace *Kent*, come not between the Dragon &
I lov'd her most, and thought to set my rest
On her kind nurcery, hence and avoide my sight?
So be my grave my peace as here I give,
Her fathers heart from her, call *France*, who stirres?
Call *Burgundy*, *Cornwell*, and *Albany*,
With my two daughters dower digest this third,
Let pride, which she cals plainnes, marrie her:
I doe invest you jointly in my powre,
Preheminence, and all the large effects
That troope with Majestie, our selfe by monthly course
With reservation of an hundred knights,
By you to be sustayn'd, shall our abode
Make with you by due turnes, onely we still retaine
The name and all the addicions to a King,
The sway, revenue, execution of the rest,
Beloved sonnes be yours, which to confirme,
This Coronet part betwixt you.

   Kent. Royall *Lear*,
Whom I have ever honor'd as my King,

[74]

Loved as my Father, as my maister followed,
As my great patron thought on in my prayers.
   Lear. The bow is bent & drawen make from the shaft,
   Kent. Let it fall rather,
Though the forke invade the region of my heart,
Be *Kent* unmannerly when *Lear* is man,
What wilt thou doe ould man, think'st thou that dutie
Shall have dread to speake, when power to flatterie bowes,
To plainnes honours bound when majesty stoops to folly,
Reverse thy doome, and in thy best consideration
Checke this hideous rashnes, answere my life
My judgement, thy yongest daughter does not love thee least,
Nor are those empty harted whose low, sound
Reverbs no hollownes.
   Lear. *Kent* on thy life no more.
   Kent. My life I never held but as a pawne
To wage against thy enemies, nor feare to lose it
Thy safty being the motive.
   Lear. Out of my sight.
   Kent. See better *Lear* and let me still remaine,
The true blanke of thine eye.
   Lear. Now by *Appollo*,
   Kent. Now by *Appollo* King thou swearest thy Gods
   Lear. Vassall, recreant.   (in vaine.
   Kent. Doe, kill thy Physicion,
And the fee bestow upon the foule disease,
Revoke thy doome, or whilst I can vent clamour
From my throat, ile tell thee thou dost evill.
   Lear. Heare me, on thy allegeance heare me?
Since thou hast sought to make us break our vow,
Which we durst never yet; and with straied pride,
To come betweene our sentence and our powre,
Which not our nature nor our place can beare,
Our potency made good, take thy reward,
Foure dayes we doe allot thee for provision,
To shield thee from diseases of the world,
And on the fift to turne thy hated backe

Upon our kingdome, if on the tenth day following,
Thy banisht truncke be found in our dominions,
The moment is thy death, away, by *Jupiter*
This shall not be revokt.   (appeare,
    Kent. Why fare thee well king, since thus thou wilt
Friendship lives hence, and banishment is here,
The Gods to their protection take the maide,
That rightly thinks and hast most justly said,
And your large speeches may your deedes approve,
That good effects may spring from wordes of love:
Thus *Kent* O Princes, bids you all adew,
Heele shape his old course in a countrie new.

Enter France and Burgundie with Gloster

    Glost. Heers *France* and *Burgundie* my noble Lord.
    Lear. My L. of *Burgundie* we first addres towards you,
Who with a King hath rivald for our daughter,
What in the least will you require in present
Dower with her, or cease your quest of love?
    Burg. Royall majesty, I crave no more then what
Your highnes offered, nor will you tender lesse?   (us
    Lear. Right noble *Burgundie*, when she was deere to
We did hold her so, but now her prise is fallen,
Sir there she stands, if ought within that little
Seeming substance, or al of it with our displeasure peec'st,
And nothing else may fitly like your grace,
Shees there, and she is yours.
    Burg. I know no answer.
    Lear. Sir will you with those infirmities she owes,
Unfriended, new adopted to our hate,
Covered with our curse, and stranger'd with our oth,
Take her or leave her.
    Burg. Pardon me royall Sir, election makes not up
On such conditions.   (me
    Lear. Then leave her sir, for by the powre that made
I tell you all her wealth, for you great King,
I would not from your love make such a stray,

To match you where I hate, therefore beseech you,
To avert you liking a more worthier way,
Then on a wretch whome nature is ashamed
Almost to acknowledge hers.
   Fra. This is most strange, that she, that even but now
Was your best object, the argument of your praise,
Balme of your age, most best, most deerest,
Should in this trice of time commit a thing,
So monstrous to dismantell so many foulds of favour,
Sure her offence must be of such unnaturall degree,
That monsters it, or you for voucht affections
Falne into taint, which to beleeve of her
Must be a faith that reason without miracle
Could never plant in me.
   Cord. I yet beseech your Majestie,
If for I want that glib and oyly Art,
To speake and purpose not, since what I well entend
Ile do't before I speake, that you may know
It is no vicious blot, murder or foulnes,
No uncleane action or dishonord step
That hath depriv'd me of your grace and favour,
But even for want of that, for which I am rich,
A still soliciting eye, and such a tongue,
As I am glad I have not, though not to have it,
Hath lost me in your liking.
   Leir. Goe to, goe to, better thou hadst not bin borne,
Then not to have pleas'd me better.
   Fran. Is it no more but this, a tardines in nature,
That often leaves the historie unspoke that it intends to
My Lord of *Burgundie*, what say you to the Lady? (do,
Love is not love when it is mingled with respects that
Aloofe from the intire point wil you have her? (stands
She is her selfe and dowre.
   Burg. Royall *Leir*, give but that portion
Which your selfe proposd, and here I take *Cordelia*
By the hand, Dutches of *Burgundie*,
   Leir. Nothing, I have sworne.

Burg. I am sory then you have so lost a father,
That you must loose a husband.

Cord. Peace be with *Burgundie*, since that respects
Of fortune are his love, I shall not be his wife.

Fran. Fairest *Cordelia* that art most rich being poore,
Most choise forsaken, and most loved despisd,
Thee and thy vertues here I ceaze upon,
Be it lawfull I take up whats cast away,
Gods, Gods! tis strange, that from their couldst neglect,
My love should kindle to inflam'd respect,
Thy dowreles daughter King throwne to thy chance,
Is Queene of us, of ours, and our faire *France*:
Not all the Dukes in watrish *Burgundie*,
Shall buy this unprizd precious maide of me,
Bid them farewell *Cordelia*, though unkind
Thou loosest here, a better where to find.

Lear. Thou hast her *France*, let her be thine,
For we have no such daughter, nor shall ever see
That face of hers againe, therefore be gone, (*Burgundy.*
Without our grace, our love, our benizon? come noble

Exit Lear and Burgundie.

Fran. Bid farewell to your sisters?

Cord. The jewels of our father,   (you are,
With washt eyes *Cordelia* leaves you, I know you what
And like a sister am most loath to call your faults
As they are named, use well our Father,
To your professed bosoms I commit him,
But yet alas stood I within his grace,
I would preferre him to a better place:
So farewell to you both?

Gonorill. Prescribe not us our duties?

Regan. Let your study be to content your Lord,
Who hath receaved you at Fortunes almes,
You have obedience scanted,
And well are worth the worth that you have wanted.

Cord. Time shal unfould what pleated cunning hides,

Who covers faults, at last shame them derides:
Well may you prosper.

Fran. Come faire *Cordelia?*   *Exit France & Cord.*

Gonor. Sister, it is not a little I have to say,
Of what most neerely appertaines to us both,
I thinke our father will hence to night.

Reg. Thats most certaine and with you, next moneth with us.

Gon. You see how full of changes his age is the observation we have made of it hath not bin little; hee alwaies loved our sister most, and with what poore judgement hee hath now cast her off, appeares too grosse.

Reg. Tis the infirmitie of his age, yet hee hath ever but slenderly knowne himselfe.

Gono. The best and soundest of his time hath bin but rash, then must we looke to receive from his age not alone the imperfection of long ingrafted condition, but therwithal unruly waywardnes, that infirme and cholericke yeares bring with them.

Rag. Such unconstant starts are we like to have from him, as this of *Kents* banishment.

Gono. There is further complement of leave taking betweene *France* and him, pray lets hit together, if our Father cary authority with such dispositions as he beares, this last surrender of his, will but offend us,

Ragan. We shall further thinke on't.

Gon. We must doe something, and it'h heate.   *Exeunt.*

Enter Bastard Solus.

Bast. Thou Nature art my Goddesse, to thy law my services are bound, wherefore should I stand in the plague of custome, and permit the curiositie of nations to deprive me, for that I am some twelve or 14. mooneshines lag of a brother, why bastard? wherfore base, when my dementions are as well compact, my mind as generous, and my shape as true as honest madams issue, why brand they us with base, base bastardie? who in the lusty stealth of nature, take more composition and feirce quality, then doth within a stale dull lyed bed, goe to the creating of a whole tribe of fops got tweene a sleepe and wake; well the legitimate *Edgar*, I must have your land, our Fathers love is to the bastard *Edmund*, as to the legitimate, well my legitimate, if this letter speede, and my invention thrive, *Edmund* the base shall tooth'legitimate: I grow, I prosper, now Gods stand up for Bastards.

Enter Gloster.

Glost. *Kent* banisht thus, and *France* in choller parted, and the King gone to night, subscribd his power, confined to exhibition, all this donne upon the gadde; *Edmund* how now what newes?

Bast. So please your Lordship, none:

Glost. Why so earnestly seeke you to put up that letter?

Bast. I know no newes my Lord.

Glost. What paper were you reading?

Bast. Nothing my Lord,

Glost. No, what needes then that terribe dispatch of it into your pocket, the qualitie of nothing hath not such need to hide it selfe, lets see, come if it bee nothing I shall not neede spectacles.

Ba. I beseech you Sir pardon me, it is a letter from my brother, that I have not all ore read, for so much as I have perused, I find it not fit for your liking.

Glost. Give me the letter sir.

Bast. I shall offend either to detaine or give it, the contents as in part I understand them, are too blame.

Glost. Lets see, lets see?

Bast. I hope for my brothers justification, he wrot this but as an essay, or tast of my vertue.   *A Letter.*

Glost. This policie of age makes the world bitter to the best of our times, keepes our fortunes from us till our oldness cannot relish them, I begin to find an idle and fond bondage in the oppression of aged tyranny, who swaies not as it hath power, but as it is suffered, come to me, that of this I may speake more, if our father would sleepe till I wakt him, you should injoy halfe his revenew for ever, and live the beloved of your brother *Edgar*.

Hum, conspiracie, slept till I wakt him, you should enjoy halfe his revenew, my sonne *Edgar*, had hee a hand to write this, a hart and braine to breed it in, when came this to you, who brought it?

Bast. It was not brought me my Lord, ther's the cunning of it, I found it throwne in at the casement of my closet.

Glost. You know the Caracter to be your brothers?

Bast. If the matter were good my Lord I durst sweare it were his but in respect, of that I would faine thinke it were not,

Glost. It is his?

Bast. It is his hand my Lord, but I hope his heart is not in the contents.

Glost. Hath he never heretofore sounded you in this busines?

Bast. Never my Lord, but I have often heard him maintaine it to be fit, that sons at perfit age, & fathers declining, his father, should be as ward to the sonne, and the sonne manage the revenew.

Glost. O villaine, villaine, his very opinion in the letter, abhorred villaine, unnaturall detested brutish villaine, worse then brutish, go sir seeke him, I apprehend him, abhominable villaine where is he?

Bast. I doe not well my Lord, if it shall please you to suspend your indignation against my brother, til you can derive from him better testimony of this intent: you should run a certaine course, where if you violently proceed against him, mistaking his purpose, it would make a great gap in your owne honour, & shake in peeces the heart of his obedience, I dare pawn downe my life for him, he hath wrote this to feele my affection to your honour, and to no further pretence of danger.

Glost. Thinke you so?

Bast. If your honour judge it meete, I will place you where you shall heare us conferre of this, and by an aurigular assurance have your satisfaction, and that without any further delay then this very evening.

Glost. He cannot be such a monster.

Bast. Nor is not sure.

Glost. To his father, that so tenderly and intirely loves him, heaven and earth! *Edmund* seeke him out, wind mee into him, I pray you frame your busines after your own wisedome, I would unstate my selfe to be in a due resolution.

Bast. I shall seeke him sir presently, convey the businesse as I shall see meanes, and acquaint you withall.

Glost. These late eclipses in the Sunne and Moone portend no good to us, though the wisedome of nature can reason thus and thus, yet nature finds it selfe scourg'd by the sequent effects, love cooles, friendship fals off, brothers divide, in Citties mutinies, in Countries discords, Pallaces treason, the bond crackt betweene sonne and father; find out this villaine *Edmund*, it shal loose thee nothing, doe it carefully, and the noble and true harted *Kent* banisht, his offence honest, strange strange!

Bast. This is the excellent foppery of the world, that when we are sicke in Fortune, often the surfeit of our owne behaviour, we make guiltie of our disasters, the Sunne, the Moone, and the Starres, as if we were Villaines by necessitie, Fooles by heavenly compulsion, Knaves, Theeves, and Trecherers by spirituall predominance, Drunkards, Lyars, and Adulterers by an enforst obedience of planitary influence, and all that wee are evill in, by a divine thrusting on, an admirable evasion of whoremaster man, to lay his gotish disposition to the charge of Starres: my Father compounded with my Mother under the Dragons taile, and my nativitie was under *Ursa major*, so that it followes, I am rough and lecherous, Fut, I should have beene that I am, had the maidenlest starre of the Firmament twinckled on

★ my bastardy *Edgar;* and out hee comes like the Catastrophe of the old Comedy, mine is villanous melancholy, with a

---

★ In the original version *Enter Edgar* appeared here, in the margin.

sith like them of Bedlam; O these eclipses doe portend these divisions.

Edgar. How now brother *Edmund,* what serious contemplation are you in?

Bast. I am thinking brother of a prediction I read this other day, what should follow these Eclipses.

Edg. Doe you busie your selfe about that?

Bast. I promise you the effects he writ of succeed unhappily, as of unnaturalnesse betweene the child and the parent, death, dearth, dissolutions of ancient amities, divisions in state, menaces and maledictions against King and nobles, needles diffidences, banishment of friends, dissipation of Cohorts, nuptial breaches, and I know not what.

Edg. How long have you beene a sectary Astronomicall?

Bast. Come, come, when saw you my father last?

Edg. Why, the night gon by.

Bast. Spake you with him?

Edg. Two houres together.

Bast. Parted you in good tearmes? found you no displeasure in him by word or countenance?

Edg. None at all.

Bast. Bethinke your selfe wherein you may have offended him, and at my intreatie, forbeare his presence, till some little time hath qualified the heat of his displeasure, which at this instant so rageth in him, that with the mischiefe, of your parson it would scarce allay.

Edg. Some villaine hath done me wrong.

Bast. Thats my feare brother, I advise you to the best, goe arm'd, I am no honest man if there bee any good meaning towards you, I have told you what I have seene & heard, but faintly, nothing like the image and horror of it, pray you away?

Edg. Shall I heare from you anon?

Bast. I doe serve you in this busines: *Exit Edgar*
A credulous Father, and a brother noble,
Whose nature is so farre from doing harmes,
That he suspects none, on whose foolish honesty

[83]

My practises ride easie, I see the busines,
Let me if not by birth, have lands by wit,
All with me's meete, that I can fashion fit.   *Exit.*

Enter Gonorill and Gentleman.

Gon. Did my Father strike my gentleman for chiding of his foole?
Gent. Yes Madam.
Gon. By day and night he wrongs me,
Every houre he flashes into one grosse crime or other
That sets us all at ods, ile not indure it,
His Knights grow ryotous, and him selfe obrayds us,
On every trifell when he returnes from hunting,
I will not speake with him, say I am sicke,
If you come slacke of former services,
You shall doe well, the fault of it ile answere.
Gent. Hee's coming Madam I heare him.
Gon. Put on what wearie negligence you please, you and your fellow servants, i'de have it come in question, if he dislike it, let him to our sister, whose mind and mine I know in that are one, not to be overruld; idle old man that still would manage those authorities that hee hath given away, now by my life old fooles are babes again, & must be us'd with checkes as flatteries, when they are seene abusd, remember what I tell you.
Gent. Very well Madam.
Gon. And let his Knights have colder looks among you, what growes of it no matter, advise your fellowes so, I would breed from hence occasions, and I shall, that I may speake, ile write straight to my sister to hould my very course, goe prepare for dinner.   *Exit.*

Enter Kent.

Kent. If but as well I other accents borrow, that can my speech defuse, my good intent may carry through it selfe to that full issue for which I raz'd my likenes, now banisht *Kent,*

[84]

if thou canst serve where thou dost stand condem'd, thy maister whom thou lovest shall find the full of labour.

Enter Lear.

Lear. Let me not stay a jot for dinner, goe get it readie, how now, what art thou?

Kent. A man Sir.

Lear. What dost thou professe? what would'st thou with us?

Kent. I doe professe to be no lesse then I seeme, to serve him truly that will put me in trust, to love him that is honest, to converse with him that is wise, and sayes little, to feare judgement, to fight when I cannot chuse, and to eate no fishe.

Lear. What art thou?

Kent. A very honest harted fellow, and as poore as the king.

Lear. If thou be as poore for a subject, as he is for a King, thar't poore enough, what would'st thou?

Kent. Service.   *Lear.* Who would'st thou serve?

Kent. You. *Lear.* Do'st thou know me fellow?

Kent. No sir, but you have that in your countenance, which I would faine call Maister.

Lear. Whats that?   *Kent.* Authoritie.

Lear. What services canst doe?

Kent. I can keepe honest counsaile, ride, run, mar a curious tale in telling it, and deliver a plaine message bluntly, that which ordinarie men are fit for, I am qualified in, and the best of me, is diligence.

Lear. How old art thou?

Kent. Not so yong to love a woman for singing, nor so old to dote on her for anything, I have yeares on my backe fortie eight.

Lear. Follow mee, thou shalt serve mee, if I like thee no worse after dinner, I will not part from thee yet, dinner, ho dinner, wher's my knave, my foole, goe you call my foole hether, you sirra whers my daughter?

Enter Steward.

[85]

Steward. So please you,

Lear. What say's the fellow there, call the clat-pole backe, whers my foole, ho I thinke the world's asleepe, how now, wher's that mungrel?

Kent. He say's my Lord, your daughter is not well.

Lear. Why came not the slave backe to mee when I cal'd him?

servant. Sir, hee answered mee in the roundest manner, hee would not. *Lear.* A would not?

servant. My Lord, I know not what the matter is, but to my judgement, your highnes is not entertained with that ceremonious affection as you were wont, ther's a great abatement, apeer's as well in the generall dependants, as in the Duke himselfe also, and your daughter. *Lear.* Ha, say'st thou so?

servant. I beseech you pardon mee my Lord, if I be mistaken, for my dutie cannot bee silent, when I thinke your highnesse wrong'd.

Lear. Thou but remember'st me of mine owne conception, I have perceived a most faint neglect of late, which I have rather blamed as mine owne jelous curiositie, then as a very pretence & purport of unkindnesse, I will looke further into't, but wher's this foole? I have not seene him this two dayes.

servant. Since my yong Ladies going into *France* sir, the foole hath much pined away.

Lear. No more of that, I have noted it, goe you and tell my daughter, I would speake with her, goe you cal hither my foole, O you sir, you sir, come you hither, who am I sir?

Steward. My Ladies Father.

Lear. My Ladies father, my Lords knave, you horeson dog, you slave, you cur.

Stew. I am none of this my Lord, I beseech you pardon me.

Lear. Doe you bandie lookes with me you rascall?

Stew. Ile not be struck my Lord,

Kent. Nor tript neither, you base football player.

Lear. I thanke thee fellow, thou serv'st me, and ile love thee.

Kent. Come sir ile teach you differences, away, away, if you will measure your lubbers length againe, tarry, but away, you have wisedome.

Lear. Now friendly knave I thanke thee, their's earnest of thy service.   *Enter Foole.*

Foole. Let me hire him too, heer's my coxcombe.

Lear. How now my pretty knave, how do'st thou?

Foole. Sirra, you were best take my coxcombe.

Kent. Why Foole?

Foole. Why for taking on's part, that's out of favour, nay and thou can'st not smile as the wind sits, thou't catch cold shortly, there take my coxcombe; why this fellow hath banisht two on's daughters, and done the third a blessing against his will, if thou follow him, thou must needs weare my coxcombe, how now nuncle, would I had two coxcombes, and two daughters.

Lear. Why my boy?

Foole. If I gave them any living, id'e keepe my coxcombs my selfe, ther's mine, beg another of thy daughters.

Lear. Take heede sirra, the whip.

Foole. Truth is a dog that must to kenell, hee must bee whipt out, when Ladie oth'e brach may stand by the fire and stincke.

Lear. A pestilent gull to mee.

Foole. Sirra ile teach thee a speech.   *Lear.* Doe.

Foole. Marke it uncle, have more then thou shewest, speake lesse then thou knowest, lend lesse then thou owest, ride more then thou goest, learne more then thou trowest, set lesse then thou throwest, leave thy drinke and thy whore, and keepe in a doore, and thou shalt have more, then two tens to a score.

Lear. This is nothing foole.

Foole. Then like the breath of an unfeed Lawyer, you gave me nothing for't, can you make no use of nothing uncle?

Lear. Why no boy, nothing can be made out of nothing.

Foole. Preethe tell him so much the rent of his land comes to, he will not beleeve a foole.

Lear. A bitter foole.

Foole. Doo'st know the difference my boy, betweene a bitter foole, and a sweete foole.

Lear. No lad, teach mee.

Foole. That Lord that counsail'd thee to give away thy land,
Come place him heere by mee, doe thou for him stand,
The sweet and bitter foole will presently appeare,
The one in motley here, the other found out there.

Lear. Do'st thou call mee foole boy?

Foole. All thy other Titles thou hast given away, that thou wast borne with.

Kent. This is not altogether foole my Lord.

Foole. No faith, Lords and great men will not let me, if I had a monopolie out, they would have part an't, and Ladies too, they will not let me have all the foole to my selfe, they'l be snatching; give me an egge Nuncle, and ile give thee two crownes.

Lear. What two crownes shall they be?

Foole. Why, after I have cut the egge in the middle and eate up the meate, the two crownes of the egge; when thou clovest thy crowne it'h middle, and gavest away both parts, thou borest thy asse at'h backe or'e the durt, thou had'st little wit in thy bald crowne, when thou gavest thy golden one away, if I speake like my selfe in this, let him be whipt that first finds it so.

Fooles had nere lesse wit in a yeare,
For wise men are growne foppish,
They know not how their wits doe weare,
Their manners are so apish.

Lear. When were you wont to be so full of songs sirra?

Foole. I have us'd it nuncle, ever since thou mad'st thy daughters thy mother, for when thou gavest them the rod, and put'st downe thine own breeches, then they for sudden joy did weep, and I for sorrow sung, that such a King should play bo-peepe, and goe the fooles among: prethe Nunckle

keepe a schoolemaster that can teach thy foole to lye, I would
faine learne to lye.

Lear. And you lye, weele have you whipt.

Foole. I marvell what kin thou and thy daughters are,
they'l have me whipt for speaking true, thou wilt have mee
whipt for lying, and sometime I am whipt for holding my
peace, I had rather be any kind of thing then a foole, and yet I
would not bee thee Nuncle, thou hast pared thy wit both
sides, & left nothing in the middle, here comes one of the
parings.

Enter Gonorill.

Lear. How now daughter, what makes that Frontlet on,
Me thinks you are too much alate it'h frowne.

Foole. Thou wast a prettie fellow when thou had'st no
need to care for her frowne, now thou art an O without a
figure, I am better then thou art now, I am a foole, thou art
nothing, yes forsooth I will hould my tongue, so your face
bids mee, though you say nothing.
Mum, mum, he that keepes neither crust nor crum,
Wearie of all, shall want some. That's a sheald pescod.

Gon. Not onely sir this, your all-licenc'd foole, but other
of your insolent retinue do hourely carpe and quarrell,
breaking forth in ranke & (not to be indured riots,) Sir I had
thought by making this well knowne unto you, to have
found a safe redres, but now grow fearefull by what your
selfe too late have spoke and done, that you protect this
course, and put on by your allowance, which if you should,
the fault would not scape censure, nor the redresse, sleepe,
which in the tender of a wholsome weale, might in their
working doe you that offence, that else were shame, that
then necessitie must call discreet proceedings.

Foole. For you trow nuncle, the hedge sparrow fed the
Cookow so long, that it had it head bit off beit young, so out
went the candle, and we were left darkling.

Lear. Are you our daughter?

Gon. Come sir, I would you would make use of that good

wisedome whereof I know you are fraught, and put away these dispositions, that of late transforme you from what you rightly are.

Foole. May not an Asse know when the cart drawes the horse, whoop *Jug* I love thee.

Lear. Doth any here know mee? why this is not *Lear*, doth *Lear* walke thus? speake thus? where are his eyes, either his notion, weaknes, or his discernings are lethergie, sleeping, or wakeing; ha! sure tis not so, who is it that can tell me who I am? *Lears* shadow? I would learne that, for by the markes of soveraintie, knowledge, and reason, I should bee false perswaded I had daughters.

Foole. Which they, will make an obedient father.

Lear. Your name faire gentlewoman?

Gon. Come sir, this admiration is much of the favour of other your new prankes, I doe beseech you understand my purposes aright, as you are old and reverend, should be wise, here do you keepe a 100. Knights and Squires, men so disordred, so deboyst and bold, that this our court infected with their manners, showes like a riotous Inne, epicurisme, and lust make more like a taverne or brothell, then a great pallace, the shame it selfe doth speake for instant remedie, be thou desired by her, that else will take the thing shee begs, a little to disquantitie your traine, and the remainder that shall still depend, to bee such men as may besort your age, that know themselves and you.

Lear. Darkenes and Devils! saddle my horses, call my traine together, degenerate bastard, ile not trouble thee, yet have I left a daughter.

Gon. You strike my people, and your disordred rabble, make servants of their betters.   *Enter Duke.*

Lear. We that too late repent's, O sir, are you come? is it your will that wee prepare any horses, ingratitude! thou marble harted fiend, more hideous when thou shewest thee in a child, then the Sea-monster, detested kite, thou lift my traine, and men of choise and rarest parts, that all particulars of dutie knowe, and in the most exact regard, support the worships of their name, O most small fault, how ugly did'st thou in *Cordelia* shewe, that like an engine wrencht my frame of nature from the fixt place, drew from my heart all love and added to the gall, O *Lear*. *Lear!* beat at this gate that let thy folly in, and thy deere judgement out, goe goe, my people?

Duke. My Lord, I am giltles as I am ignorant.

Leir. It may be so my Lord, harke *Nature*, heare deere Goddesse, suspend thy purpose, if thou did'st intend to make this creature fruitful into her wombe, convey sterility, drie up in hir the organs of increase, and from her derogate body never spring a babe to honour her, if shee must teeme, create her childe of spleene, that it may live and bee a thourt disvetur'd torment to her, let it stampe wrinckles in her brow of youth, with accent teares, fret channels in her cheeks, turne all her mothers paines and benefits to laughter and contempt, that shee may feele, that she may feele, how sharper then a serpents tooth it is, to have a thanklesse child, goe, goe, my people?

Duke. Now Gods that we adore, whereof comes this!

Gon. Never afflict your selfe to know the cause, but let his disposition have that scope that dotage gives it.

Lear. What, fiftie of my followers at a clap, within a fortnight?

Duke. What is the matter sir?

Lear. Ile tell thee, life and death! I am asham'd that thou hast power to shake my manhood thus, that these hot teares that breake from me perforce should make the worst blasts and fogs upon the untented woundings of a fatherscursse, pierce every sence about the old fond eyes, beweepe this cause againe, ile pluck you out, & you cast with the waters that you make to temper clay, yea, is't come to this? yet have I left a daughter, whom I am sure is kind and comfortable, when shee shall heare this of thee, with her nailes shee'l flea thy wolvish visage, thou shalt find that ile resume the shape, which thou dost thinke I have cast off for ever, thou shalt I warrant thee.

Gon. Doe you marke that my Lord?

[91]

Duke. I cannot bee so partiall *Gonorill* to the great love I beare you,

Gon. Come sir no more, you, more knave then foole, after your master?

Foole. Nunckle *Lear*, Nunckle *Lear*, tary and take the foole with a fox when one has caught her, and such a daughter should sure to the slaughter, if my cap would buy a halter, so the foole followes after.

Gon. What *Oswald*, ho. *Oswald*. Here Madam.

Gon. What have you writ this letter to my sister?

Osw. Yes Madam.

Gon. Take you some company, and away to horse, informe her full of my particular feares, and thereto add such reasons of your owne, as may compact it more, get you gon & hasten your returne now my Lord, this milkie gentlenes and course of yours though I dislike not, yet under pardon y'are much more attaskt for want of wisedome, then praise for harmfull mildnes.

Duke. How farre your eyes may pearce I cannot tell, striving to better ought, we marre whats well.

Gon. Nay then.   *Duke.* Well, well, the event,   *Exeunt*

Enter Lear.

Lear. Goe you before to *Gloster* with these letters, acquaint my daughter no further with any thing you know, then comes from her demand out of the letter, if your diligence be not speedie, I shall be there before you.

Kent. I will not sleepe my Lord, till I have delivered your letter.   *Exit*

Foole. If a mans braines where in his heeles, wert not in danger of kibes?   *Lear.* I boy.

Foole. Then I prethe be mery, thy wit shal nere goe slipshod.

Lear. Ha ha ha.

Foole. Shalt see thy other daughter will use thee kindly, for though shees as like this, as a crab is like an apple, yet I con, what I can tel.

Lear. Why what canst thou tell my boy?

Foole. Sheel tast as like this, as a crab doth to a crab, thou canst not tell why ones nose stande in the midle of his face?

Lear. No.

Foole. Why, to keep his eyes on either side's nose, that what a man cannot smell out, a may spie into.

Lear. I did her wrong.

Foole. Canst tell how an Oyster makes his shell. *Lear.* No.

Foole. Nor I neither, but I can tell why a snayle has a house.

Lear. Why?

Foole. Why, to put his head in, not to give it away to his daughter, and leave his hornes without a case.

Lear. I will forget my nature, so kind a father; be my horses readie?

Foole. Thy Asses are gone about them, the reason why the seven starres are no more then seven, is a prettie reason.

Lear. Because they are not eight.

Foole. Yes thou wouldst make a good foole.

Lear. To tak't againe perforce, Monster, ingratitude!

Fool. If thou wert my foole Nunckle, id'e have thee beaten for being old before thy time.

Lear. Hows that?

Foole. Thou shouldst not have beene old, before thou hadst beene wise.

Lear. O let me not be mad sweet heaven! I would not be mad, keepe me in temper, I would not be mad, are the horses readie?

Servant. Readie my Lord. *Lear.* Come boy. *Exit.*

Foole. Shee that is maide now, and laughs at my departure, Shall not be maide long, except things be cut shorter. *Exit*

Enter Bast. and Curan meeting

Bast. Save thee *Curan.*

Curan. And you Sir, I have beene with your father, and given him notice, that the Duke of *Cornwall* and his Dutches will bee here with him tonight.

Bast. How comes that?

Curan. Nay, I know not, you have heard of the newes abroad, I meane the whisperd ones, for there are yet but eare-bussing arguments.

Bast. Not, I pray you what are they?

Curan. Have you heard of no likely warres towards, twixt the two Dukes of *Cornwall* and *Albany?*

Bast. Not a word.

Curan. You may then in time, fare you well sir.

Bast. The Duke be here to night! the better best, this weaves
★ it selfe perforce into my busines, my father hath set gard to take my brother, and I have one thing of a quesie question, which must ask breefnes and fortune helpe; brother, a word, discend brother I say, my father watches, O flie this place, intelligence is given where you are hid, you have now the good advantage of the night, have you not spoken gainst the Duke of *Cornwall* ought, hee's coming hether now in the night, it'h hast, and *Regan* with him, have you nothing said upon his partie against the Duke of *Albany*, advise your———

Edg. I am sure on't not a word.

Bast. I heare my father coming, pardon me in craving, I must draw my sword upon you, seeme to defend your selfe, now quit you well, yeeld, come before my father, light here, here, flie brother flie, torches, torches, so farwell; some bloud drawne on mee would beget opinion of my more fierce indevour, I have seene drunckards doe more then this in sport, father, father, stop, stop, no, helpe?   *Enter Glost.*

Glost. Now *Edmund* where is the villaine?

Bast. Here stood he in the darke, his sharpe sword out, warbling of wicked charms, conjuring the Moone to stand's auspicious Mistris.   *Glost.* But where is he?

Bast. Looke sir, I bleed.

Glost. Where is the villaine *Edmund?*

Bast. Fled this way sir, when by no meanes he could———

Glost. Pursue him, go after, by no meanes, what?

★ In the original version *Enter Edgar* appeared here, in the margin.

Bast. Perswade me to the murder of your Lordship, but that I told him the revengive Gods, gainst Paracides did all their thunders bend, spoke with how many fould and strong a bond the child was bound to the father, sir in a fine, seeing how loathly opposite I stood, to his unnaturall purpose, with fell motion with his prepared sword, hee charges home my unprovided body, lancht mine arme, but when he saw my best alarumd spirits, bould in the quarrels, rights, rousd to the encounter, or whether gasted by the noyse I made, but sodainly he fled.

Glost. Let him flie farre, not in this land shall hee remaine uncaught and found, dispatch the noble Duke my maister, my worthy Arch and Patron, comes to night, by his authoritie I will proclaime it, that he which finds him shall deserve our thankes, bringing the murderous caytife to the stake, hee that conceals him, death.

Bast. When I disswaded him from his intent, and found him pight to doe it, with curst speech I threatned to discover him, he replyed, thou unpossessing Bastard, dost thou thinke, if I would stand against thee, could the reposure of any trust, vertue, or worth in thee make thy words fayth'd? no. what I should denie, as this I would, I, though thou didst produce my very character, id'e turne it all to thy suggestion, plot, and damned pretence, and thou must make a dullard of the world, if they not thought the profits of my death, were very pregnant and potentiall spurres to make thee seeke it.

Glost. Strong and fastned villaine, would he denie his letter, I never got him, harke the Dukes trumpets, I know not why he comes, all Ports ile barre, the villaine shall not scape, the Duke must grant mee that, besides, his picture I will send farre and neere, that all the kingdome may have note of him, and of my land loyall and naturall boy, ile worke the meanes to make thee capable.

Enter the Duke of Cornwall.

Corn. How now my noble friend, since I came hether, which I can call but now, I have heard strange newes.

[95]

Reg. If it be true, all vengeance comes too short which can pursue the offender, how dost my Lord?

Glost. Madam my old heart is crackt, is crackt.

Reg. What, did my fathers godson seeke your life? he whom my father named your *Edgar*?

Glost. I Ladie, Ladie, shame would have it hid.

Reg. Was he not companion with the ryotous knights, that tends upon my father?

Glost. I know not Madam, tis too bad, too bad.

Bast. Yes Madam, he was.

Reg. No marvaile then though he were ill affected,
Tis they have put him on the old mans death,
To have the wast and spoyle of his revenues:
I have this present evening from my sister,
Beene well inform'd of them, and with such cautions,
That if they come to sojourne at my house, ile not be there.

Duke. Nor I, assure thee *Regan*; *Edmund,* I heard that you have shewen your father a child-like office.

Bast. Twas my dutie Sir.

Glost. He did betray his practice, and received
This hurt you see, striving to apprehend him.

Duke. Is he pursued?   *Glost.* I my good Lord.

Duke. If he be taken, he shall never more be feard of doing harme, make your own purpose how in my strength you please, for you *Edmund*, whose vertue and obedience, doth this instant so much commend it selfe, you shall bee ours, natures of such deepe trust, wee shall much need you, we first seaze on.

Bast. I shall serve you truly, how ever else.

Glost. For him I thanke your grace.

Duke. You know not why we came to visit you?

Regan. Thus out of season, threatning darke ey'd night,
Ocasions noble *Gloster* of some poyse,
Wherein we must have use of your advise,
Our Father he hath writ, so hath our sister,
Of diferences, which I lest thought it fit,
To answer from our home, the several messengers

From hence attend dispatch, our good old friend,
Lay comforts to your bosome, & bestow your needfull councell
To our busines, which craves the instant use.   *Exeunt*
  Glost. I serve you Madam, your Graces are right welcome.

Enter Kent, and Steward.

Steward. Good even to thee friend, art of the house?
Kent. I.   *Stew.* Where may we set our horses?
Kent. It'h mire.   *Stew.* Prethee if thou love me, tell me.
Kent. I love thee not.   *Stew.* Why then I care not for thee.
Kent. If I had thee in Lipsburie pinfold, I would make thee
care for mee.
Stew. Why dost thou use me thus? I know thee not.
Kent. Fellow I know thee.
Stew. What dost thou know me for?
Kent. A knave, a rascall, an eater of broken meates, a base,
proud, shallow, beggerly, three shewted hundred pound,
filthy worsted-stocken knave, a lilly lyver'd action taking
knave, a whorson glassegazing superfinicall rogue, one
truncke inheriting slave, one that would'st bee a baud in way
of good service, and art nothing but the composition of a
knave, begger, coward, pander, and the sonne and heire of a
mungrell bitch, whom I will beat into clamorous whyning, if
thou denie the least sillable of the addition.
Stew. What a monstrous fellow art thou, thus to raile on
one, that's neither knowne of thee, nor knowes thee.
Kent. What a brazen fac't varlet art thou, to deny thou
knowest mee, is it two dayes agoe since I beat thee, and tript
up thy heeles before the King? draw you rogue, for though it
be night the Moone shines, ile make a sop of the moone-
shine a'you, draw you whorson cullyonly barber-munger,
draw?
Stew. Away, I have nothing to doe with thee.
Kent. Draw you rascall, you bring letters against the
King, and take Vanitie the puppets part, against the royaltie
of her father, draw you rogue or ile so carbonado your
shankes, draw you rascall, come your wayes.

[97]

Stew. Helpe, ho, murther, helpe.

Kent. Strike you slave, stand rogue, stand you neate slave, strike? *Stew.* Helpe, ho, murther, helpe.

Enter Edmund with his rapier drawne, Gloster the Duke and Dutchesse.

Bast. How now, whats the matter?

Kent. With you goodman boy, and you please come, ile fleash you, come on yong maister.

Glost. Weapons, armes, whats the matter here?

Duke. Keepe peace upon your lives, hee dies that strikes againe, what's the matter?

Reg. The messengers from our sister, and the King.

Duke. Whats your difference, speake?

Stew. I am scarse in breath my Lord.

Kent. No marvaile you have so bestir'd your valour, you cowardly rascall, nature disclaimes in thee, a Tayler made thee.

Duke. Thou art a strange fellow, a Taylor make a man.

Kent. I, a Tayler sir; a Stone-cutter, or a Painter could not have made him so ill, though hee had beene but two houres at the trade.

Glost. Speake yet, how grew your quarrell?

Stew. This ancient ruffen sir, whose life I have spar'd at sute of his gray-beard.

Kent. Thou whorson Zedd, thou unnecessarie letter, my Lord if you'l give mee leave, I will tread this unboulted villaine into morter, and daube the walles of a jaques with him, spare my gray beard you wagtayle.

Duke. Peace sir, you beastly Knave you have no reverence.

Kent. Yes sir, but anger has a priviledge.

Duke. Why art thou angry?

Kent. That such a slave as this should weare a sword,
That weares no honesty, such smiling roges as these,
Like Rats oft bite those cordes in twaine,
Which are to intrench, to inloose smooth every passion
That in the natures of their Lords rebell,

[98]

Bring oyle to stir, snow to their colder-moods,
Reneag, affirme, and turne their halcion beakes
With every gale and varie of their maisters,   (epeliptick
Knowing nought like dayes but following, a plague upon your
Visage, smoyle you my speeches, as I were a foole?
Goose and I had you upon Sarum plaine,
Id'e send you cackling home to Camulet.,

    Duke. What art thou mad old fellow?

    Glost. How fell you out, say that?

    Kent. No contraries hold more, antipathy,
Then I and such a knave.

    Duke. Why dost thou call him knave, what's his offence.

    Kent. His countenance likes me not.

    Duke. No more perchance does mine, or his, or hers.

    Kent. Sir tis my occupation to be plaine,
I have seene better faces in my time
That stands on any shoulder that I see
Before me at this instant.

    Duke. This is a fellow who having beene praysd
For bluntnes doth affect a sawcy ruffines,
And constraines the garb quite from his nature,
He cannot flatter he, he must be plaine,
He must speake truth, and they will tak't so,
If not he's plaine, these kind of knaves I know
Which in this plainnes harbour more craft,
And more corrupter ends, then twentie silly ducking
Observants, that stretch their duties nisely.

    Kent. Sir in good sooth, or in sincere veritie,
Under the allowance of your graund aspect.
Whose influence like the wreath of radient fire
In flitkering *Phœbus* front.

    Duke. What mean'st thou by this?

    Kent. To goe out of my dialogue which you discommend
so much, I know sir, I am no flatterer, he that beguild you in
a plain accent, was a plaine knave, which for my part I will
not bee, though I should win your displeasure, to intreat mee
too't.

[99]

Duke. What's the offence you gave him?

Stew. I never gave him any, it pleas'd the King his maister
Very late to strike at me upon his misconstruction,
When he conjunct and flattering his displeasure
Tript me behind, being downe, insulted, rayld,
And put upon him such a deale of man, that,
That worthied him, got prayses of the King,
For him attempting who was selfe subdued,
And in the flechuent of this dread exploit,
Drew on me here againe.

Kent. None of these roges & cowards but *A'Jax* is their
foole.

Duke. Bring forth the stockes ho?
You stubburne miscreant knave, you reverent bragart,
Weele teach you.

Kent. I am too old to learne, call not your stockes for me,
I serve the King, on whose imployments I was sent to you,
You should doe small respect, shew too bold malice
Against the Grace and person of my maister,
Stopping his messenger.

Duke. Fetch forth the stockes? as I have life and honour,
There shall he sit till noone.

Reg. Till noone, till night my Lord, and all night too.

Kent. Why Madam, if I were your fathers dogge, you
could not use me so.

Reg. Sir being his knave, I will.

Duke. This is a fellow of the selfe same nature,
Our sister speake of, come bring away the stockes?

Glost. Let me beseech your Grace not to doe so,
His fault is much, and the good King his maister
Will check him for't, your purpost low correction
Is such, as basest and temnest wretches for pilfrings
And most common trespasses are punisht with,
The King must take it ill, that hee's so slightly valued
In his messenger, should have him thus restrained.

Duke. Ile answer that.

Reg. My sister may receive it much more worse,
To have her Gentlemen abus'd, assalted
For following her affaires, put in his legges,
Come my good Lord away?

Glost. I am sory for thee friend, tis the Dukes pleasure,
Whose disposition all the world well knowes
Will not be rubd nor stopt, ile intreat for thee.

Kent. Pray you doe not sir, I have watcht and travaild
Sometime I shal sleepe ont, the rest ile whistle,   (hard,
A good mans fortune may grow out at heeles,
Give you good morrow.

Glost. The Dukes to blame in this, twill be ill tooke.

Kent. Good King that must approve the common saw,
Thou out of heavens benediction comest
To the warme Sunne.
Approach thou beacon to this under gloabe,
That by thy comfortable beames I may
Peruse this letter, nothing almost sees my wracke
But miserie, I know tis from *Cordelia*,
Who hath most fortunately bin informed
Of my obscured course, and shall find time
From this enormious state, seeking to give
Losses their remedies, all wearie and overwatch
Take vantage heavie eyes not to behold
This shamefull lodging, Fortune goodnight,
Smile, once more turne thy wheele.   *sleepes.*

Enter Edgar.

Edg. I heare my selfe proclaim'd,
And by the happie hollow of a tree
Escapt the hunt, no Port is free, no place
That guard, and most unusuall vigilence
Dost not attend my taking while I may scape,
I will preserve my selfe, and am bethought
To take the basest and most poorest shape,
That ever penury in contempt of man,
Brought neare to beast, my face ile grime with filth,

Blanket my loynes, else all my haire with knots,
And with presented nakednes outface,
The wind, and persecution of the skie,
The Countrie gives me proofe and president
Of Bedlam beggers, who with roring voyces,
Strike in their numb'd and mortified bare armes,
Pins, wodden prickes, nayles, sprigs of rosemary,
And with this horrible object from low service,
Poore pelting villages, sheep-coates, and milles,
Sometime with lunaticke bans, sometime with prayers
Enforce their charitie, poore *Turlygod*, poore *Tom*,
That's something yet, *Edgar* I nothing am.   *Exit*

Enter King.

   Lear. Tis strange that they should so depart from
And not send backe my messenger.   (hence,
   Knight. As I learn'd, the night before there was
No purpose of his remove.
   Kent. Hayle to thee noble maister.
   Lear. How, mak'st thou this shame thy pastime?
   Foole. Ha ha, looke he weares crewell garters,
Horses are tide by the heeles, dogges and beares
Byt'h necke, munkies bit'h loynes, and men
Byt'h legges, when a mans over lusty at legs,
Then he weares wooden neatherstockes.
   Lear. What's he, that hath so much thy place mistooke to
set thee here?
   Kent. It is both he and shee, your sonne & daugter.
   Lear. No.   *Kent.* Yes.
   Lear. No I say,   *Kent.* I say yea.
   Lear. No no, they would not.   *Kent.* Yes they have.
   Lear. By *Jupiter* I sweare no, they durst not do't,
They would not, could not do't, tis worse then murder,
To doe upon respect such violent outrage,
Resolve me with all modest hast, which way
Thou may'st deserve, or they purpose this usage,
Coming from us.

Kent. My Lord, when at their home
I did commend your highnes letters to them,
Ere I was risen from the place that shewed
My dutie kneeling, came there a reeking Post,
Stewd in his hast, halfe breathles, panting forth
From *Gonorill* his mistris, salutations,
Delivered letters spite of intermission,
Which presently they read, on whose contents
They summond up their men, straight tooke horse,
Commanded me to follow, and attend the leasure
Of their answere, gave me cold lookes,
And meeting here the other messenger,
Whose welcome I perceav'd had poyson'd mine,
Being the very fellow that of late
Display'd so sawcily against your Highnes,
Having more man then wit about me drew,
He raised the house with loud and coward cries,
Your sonne and daughter found this trespas worth
This shame which here it suffers.

Lear. O how this mother swels up toward my hart,
Historica passio downe thou climing sorrow,
Thy element's below, where is this daughter?

Kent. With the Earle sir within,

Lear. Follow me not, stay there?

Knight. Made you no more offence then what you speake of?

Kent. No, how chance the King comes with so small a traine?

Foole. And thou hadst beene set in the stockes for that question, thou ha'dst well deserved it.

Kent. Why foole?

Foole. Weele set thee to schoole to an Ant, to teach thee ther's no labouring in the winter, all that follow their noses, are led by their eyes, but blind men, and ther's not a nose among a 100. but can smell him thats stincking, let goe thy hold when a great wheele runs downe a hill, least it breake thy necke with following it, but the great one that goes up the hill, let him draw thee after, when a wise man gives thee better councell, give mee mine againe, I would have none but knaves follow it, since a foole gives it.

    That Sir that serves for gaine,
    And followes but for forme:
    Will packe when it begin to raine,
    And leave thee in the storme.
    But I will tarie, the foole will stay,
    And let the wise man flie:
    The knave turnes foole that runs away,
    The foole no knave perdy.
Kent. Where learnt you this foole?
Foole. Not in the stockes.

Enter Lear and Gloster.

Lear. Denie to speake with mee, th'are sicke, th'are
They traveled hard to night, meare Justice,   (weary,
I the Images of revolt and flying off,
Fetch mee a better answere.
    Glost. My deere Lord, you know the fierie qualitie of the
Duke, how unremoveable and fixt he is in his owne Course.
    Lear. Vengeance, death, plague, confusion, what fierie
quality, why *Gloster, Gloster,* id'e speake with the Duke of
Cornewall, and his wife.
    Glost. I my good Lord.
    Lear. The King would speak with *Cornewal,* the deare father
Would with his daughter speake, commands her service,
Fierie Duke, tell the hot Duke that *Lear,*
No but not yet may be he is not well,
Infirmitie doth still neglect all office, where to our health
Is bound, we are not our selves, when nature being oprest
Command the mind to suffer with the bodie ile forebeare,
And am fallen out with with my more hedier will,
To take the indispos'd and sickly fit, for the sound man,
Death on my state, wherfore should he sit here?
This act perswades me, that this remotion of the Duke
Is practise, only give me my servant forth,   (& her
Tell the Duke and's wife, Ile speake with them

[104]

Now presently, bid them come forth and heare me,
Or at their chamber doore ile beat the drum,
Till it cry sleepe to death.

   Glost. I would have all well betwixt you.

   Lear. O my heart, my heart.

   Foole. Cry to it Nunckle, as the Cokney did to the eeles,
when she put um it'h pâst alive, she rapt um ath coxcombs
with a stick, and cryed downe wantons downe, twas her
brother, that in pure kindnes to his horse buttered his hay.

Enter Duke and Regan.

   Lear. Good morrow to you both.

   Duke. Hayle to your Grace.

   Reg. I am glad to see your highnes.

   Lear. Regan I thinke you are, I know what reason
I have to thinke so, if thou shouldst not be glad,
I would divorse me from thy mothers tombe
Sepulchring an adultresse yea are you free?
Some other time for that. Beloved *Regan,*
Thy sister is naught, oh *Regan* she hath tyed,
Sharpe tooth'd unkindnes, like a vulture heare,
I can scarce speake to thee, thout not beleeve,
Of how deprived a qualitie, O *Regan.*

   Reg. I pray sir take patience, I have hope
You lesse know how to value her desert,
Then she to slacke her dutie.

   Lear. My cursses on her.

   Reg. O Sir you are old,   (fine,
Nature on you standes on the very verge of her con-
You should be rul'd and led by some discretion,
That discernes your state better then you your selfe,
Therfore I pray that to our sister, you do make returne,
Say you have wrong'd her Sir?

   Lear. Aske her forgivenes,
Doe you marke how this becomes the house,
Deare daughter, I confesse that I am old,
Age is unnecessarie, on my knees I beg,

[105]

That you'l vouchsafe me rayment, bed and food.

Reg. Good sir no more, these are unsightly tricks,
Returne you to my sister.

Lear. No *Regan,*
She hath abated me of halfe my traine,
Lookt blacke upon me, strooke mee with her tongue
Most Serpent like upon the very heart,   (top,
All the stor'd vengeances of heaven fall on her ingratful
Strike her yong bones, you taking ayrs with lamenes.

Duke. Fie fie sir.
You nimble lightnings dart your blinding flames,
Into her scornfull eyes, infect her beautie,
You Fen suckt fogs, drawne by the powrefull Sunne,
To fall and blast her pride.

Reg. O the blest Gods, so will you wish on me,
When the rash mood---

Lear. No *Regan,* thou shalt never have my curse,
The tender hested nature shall not give the or'e   (burne
To harshnes, her eies are fierce, but thine do comfort & not
Tis not in thee to grudge my pleasures, to cut off my
To bandy hasty words, to scant my sizes,   (traine,
And in conclusion, to oppose the bolt
Against my coming in, thou better knowest,
The offices of nature, bond of child-hood,
Effects of curtesie, dues of gratitude,
Thy halfe of the kingdome, hast thou not forgot
Wherein I thee indow'd.

Reg. Good sir too'th purpose.

Lear. Who put my man i'th stockes?

Duke. What trumpets that?   *Enter Steward.*

Reg. I know't my sisters, this approves her letters,
That she would soone be here, is your Lady come?

Lear. This is a slave, whose easie borrowed pride
Dwels in the fickle grace of her, a followes,
Out varlet, from my sight.

Duke. What meanes your Grace?   *Enter Gon.*

Gon. Who struck my servant, *Regan* I have good hope

Thou didst not know ant.

 Lear. Who comes here? O heavens!
If you doe love old men, if you sweet sway allow
Obedience, if your selves are old, make it your cause,
Send downe and take my part,
Art not asham'd to looke upon this beard?
O *Regan* wilt thou take her by the hand?

 Gon. Why not by the hand sir, how have I offended?
Als not offence that indiscretion finds,
And dotage tearmes so.

 Lear. O sides you are too tough,
Will you yet hold? how came my man it'h stockes?

 Duke. I set him there sir, but his owne disorders
Deserv'd much lesse advancement,

 Lear. You, did you?

 Reg. I pray you father being weake seeme so,
If till the expiration of your moneth,
You will returne and sojorne with my sister,
Dismissing halfe your traine, come then to me,
I am now from home, and out of that provision,
Which shall be needful for your entertainment.

 Lear. Returne to her, and fiftie men dismist,
No rather I abjure all roofes, and chuse
To wage against the enmitie of the Ayre,
To be a Comrade with the Woolfe and owle,
Necessities sharpe pinch, returne with her,
Why the hot bloud in *France*, that dowerles
Tooke our yongest borne, I could as well be brought
To knee his throne, and Squire-like pension bag,
To keepe base life afoot, returne with her,
Perswade me rather to be slave and sumter
To this detested groome.

 Gon. At your choise sir.

 Lear. Now I prithee daughter do not make me mad,
I will not trouble thee my child, farewell,
Wee'le no more meete, no more see one another.
But yet thou art my flesh, my bloud, my daughter,

Or rather a disease that lies within my flesh,
Which I must needs call mine, thou art a bile,
A plague sore, an imbossed carbuncle in my
Corrupted bloud, but Ile not chide thee,
Let shame come when it will, I doe not call it,
I doe not bid the thunder bearer shoote,
Nor tell tailes of thee to high Judging *Jove*,
Mend when thou canst, be better at thy leasure,
I can be patient, I can stay with *Regan*,
I and my hundred Knights.

   Reg. Not altogether so sir, I looke not for you yet,
Nor am provided for your fit welcome,
Give eare sir to my sister, for those
That mingle reason with your passion,
Must be content to thinke you are old, and so,
But she knowes what shee does.

   Lear. Is this well spoken now?

   Reg. I dare avouch it sir, what fiftie followers,
Is it not well, what should you need of more,
Yea or so many, sith that both charge and danger
Speakes gainst so great a number, how in a house
Should many people under two commands
Hold amytie, tis hard, almost impossible.

   Gon. Why might not you my Lord receive attendance
From those that she cals servants, or from mine?

   Reg. Why not my Lord? if then they chanc'st to slacke you,
We could controwle them, if you will come to me,
For now I spie a danger, I intreat you,
To bring but five and twentie, to no more
Will I give place or notice.

   Lear. I gave you all.

   Reg. And in good time you gave it.

   Lear. Made you my guardians, my depositaries,
But kept a reservation to be followed
With such a number, what, must I come to you
With five and twentie, *Regan* said you so?

   Reg. And speak't againe my Lord, no more with me.

Lea. Those wicked creatures yet do seem wel favor'd
When others are more wicked, not being the worst
Stands in some ranke of prayse, Ile goe with thee,
Thy fifty yet doth double five and twentie,
And thou art twice her love.
   Gon. Heare me my Lord,
What need you five and twentie, tenne, or five,
To follow in a house, where twise so many
Have a commaund to tend you.
   Regan. What needes one?
   Lear. O reason not the deed, our basest beggers,
Are in the poorest thing superfluous,
Allow not nature more then nature needes,
Mans life as cheape as beasts, thou art a Lady,
If onely to goe warme were gorgeous,
Why nature needes not, what thou gorgeous wearest
Which scarcely keepes thee warme, but for true need,
You heavens give me that patience, patience I need,
You see me here (you Gods) a poore old fellow,
As full of greefe as age, wretched in both,
If it be you that stirres these daughters hearts
Against their Father, foole me not to much,
To beare it lamely, touch me with noble anger,
O let not womens weapons, water drops
Stayne my mans cheekes, no you unnaturall hags,
I will have such revenges on you both,
That all the world shall, I will doe such things,
What they are yet I know not, but they shal be
The terrors of the earth, you thinke ile weepe,
No ile not weepe, I have full cause of weeping,
But this heart shall breake, in a 100. thousand flowes
Or ere ile weepe, O foole I shall goe mad,

   Exeunt Lear, Leister, Kent, and Foole.

   Duke. Let us withdraw, twill be a storme.
   Reg. This house is little the old man and his people,
Cannot be well bestowed.

Gon. Tis his own blame hath put himselfe from rest,
And must needs tast his folly.

Reg. For his particuler, ile receive him gladly,
But not one follower.

Duke. So am I puspos'd, where is my Lord of *Gloster? Enter Glo*

Reg. Followed the old man forth, he is return'd.

Glo. The King is in high rage, & wil I know not whe-

Re. Tis good to give him way, he leads himselfe. (ther.

Gon. My Lord, intreat him by no meanes to stay.

Glo. Alack the night comes on, and the bleak winds
Do sorely ruffel, for many miles about ther's not a bush.

Reg. O sir, to wilfull men
The injuries that they themselves procure,
Must be their schoolemasters, shut up your doores,
He is attended with a desperate traine,
And what they may incense him to, being apt,
To have his eare abusd, wisedome bids feare.

Duke. Shut up your doores my Lord, tis a wild night,
My *Reg* counsails well, come out at'h storme.   *Exeunt.*

Enter Kent and a Gentleman at severall doores.

Kent. Whats here beside foule weather?

Gent. One minded like the weather most unquietly.

Kent. I know you, whers the King?

Gent. Contending with the fretfull element,
Bids the wind blow the earth into the sea,
Or swell the curled waters bove the maine   (haire,
That things might change or cease, teares his white
Which the impetuous blasts with eyles rage
Catch in their furie, and make nothing of,
Strives in his little world of man to outscorne,
The too and fro conflicting wind and raine,
This night wherin the cub-drawne Beare would couch,
The Lyon, and the belly pinched Wolfe
Keepe their furre dry, unbonneted he runnes,
And bids what will take all.

Kent. But who is with him?

[110]

Gent. None but the foole, who labours to out-jest
His heart strooke injuries.

Kent. Sir I doe know you,
And dare upon the warrant of my Arte,
Commend a deare thing to you, there is division,
Although as yet the face of it be cover'd,
With mutuall cunning, twixt *Albany* and *Cornwall*
But true it is, from *France* there comes a power
Into this scattered kingdome, who alreadie wise in our
Have secret feet in some of our best Ports, (negligence,
And are at point to shew their open banner
Now to you, if on my credit you dare build so farre,
To make your speed to Dover, you shall find
Some that will thanke you, making just report
Of how unnaturall and bemadding sorrow
The King hath cause to plaine,
I am a Gentleman of blood and breeding,
And from some knowledge and assurance,
Offer this office to you.

Gent. I will talke farther with you.

Kent. No doe not,
For confirmation that I much more
Then my out-wall, open this purse and take
What it containes, if you shall see *Cordelia*,
As feare not but you shall, shew her this ring,
And she will tell you who your fellow is,
That yet you doe not know, fie on this storme,
I will goe seeke the King.

Gent. Give me your hand, have you no more to say?

Kent. Few words but to effect more then all yet:
That when we have found the King.
Ile this way, you that, he that first lights
On him, hollow the other.   *Exeunt.*

Enter Lear and Foole.

Lear. Blow wind & cracke your cheekes, rage, blow
You caterickes, & Hircanios spout till you have drencht,

The steeples drown'd the cockes, you sulpherous and
Thought executing fires, vaunt-currers to
Oke-cleaving thunderboults, singe my white head,
And thou all shaking thunder, smite flat
The thicke Rotunditie of the world, cracke natures
Mold, all Germains spill at once that make
Ingratefull man.

    Foole. O Nunckle, Court holy water in a drie house
Is better then this raine water out a doore,
Good Nunckle in, and aske thy daughters blessing,
Heers a night pities nether wise man nor foole.

    Lear. Rumble thy belly full, spit fire, spout raine,
Nor raine, wind, thunder, fire, are my daughters,
I taske not you you elements with unkindnes,
I never gave you kingdome, cald you children,
You owe me no subscription, why then let fall your horrible
Here I stand your slave, a poore infirme weak &   (plesure
Despis'd ould man, but yet I call you servile
Ministers, that have with 2. pernitious daughters join'd
Your high engendred battel gainst a head so old & white
As this, O tis foule.

    Foole. Hee that has a house to put his head in, has a good
headpeece, the Codpeece that will house before the head, has
any the head and hee shall lowse, so beggers mary many, the
man that makes his toe, what hee his heart should make, shall
have a corne cry woe, and turne his sleepe to wake, for there
was never yet faire woman but shee made mouthes in a
glasse.

    Lear. No I will be the patterne of all patience   *Enter Kent.*
I will say nothing.

    Kent. Whose there?

    Foole. Marry heers Grace, & a codpis, that's a wiseman
and a foole.

    Kent. Alas sir, sit you here?
Things that love night, love not such nights as these,
The wrathfull Skies gallow, the very wanderer of the
Darke, and makes them keepe their caves,

Since I was man, such sheets of fire,
Such bursts of horred thunder, such grones of
Roaring winde, and rayne, I ne're remember
To have heard, mans nature cannot cary
The affliction, nor the force.

    Lear. Let the great Gods that keepe this dreadful
Powther ore our heades, find out their enemies now,
Tremble thou wretch that hast within thee
Undivulged crimes, unwhipt of Justice,
Hide thee thou bloudy hand, thou perjur'd, and
Thou simular man of vertue that art incestious,
Caytife in peeces shake, that under covert
And convenient seeming, hast practised on mans life,
Close pent up guilts, rive your concealed centers,
And cry these dreadfull summoners grace,
I am a man more sind against their sinning.

    Kent. Alacke bare headed, gracious my Lord, hard by here
is a hovell, some friendship will it lend you gainst the
tempest, repose you there, whilst I to this hard house, more
hard then is the stone where of tis rais'd, which even but now
demaunding after me, denide me to come in, returne and
force their scanted curtesie.

    Lear. My wit begins to turne,
Come on my boy, how dost my boy, art cold?
I am cold my selfe, where is this straw my fellow,
The art of our necessities is strange that can,
Make vild things precious, come you hovell poore,
Foole and knave, I have one part of my heart
That sorrowes yet for thee.

    Foole. Hee that has a little tine witte, with hey ho the wind
and the raine, must make content with his fortunes fit, for the
raine, it raineth every day.

    Lear. True my good boy, come bring us to this hovell?

        Enter Gloster and the Bastard with lights.

    Glost. Alacke alacke *Edmund* I like not this,
Unnaturall dealing when I desir'd their leave

[113]

That I might pitty him, they tooke me from me
The use of mine owne house, charg'd me on paine
Of their displeasure, neither to speake of him,
Intreat for him, nor any way sustaine him.
  Bast. Most savage and unnaturall.   (the Dukes,
  Glost. Go toe say you nothing, ther's a division betwixt
And a worse matter then that, I have received
A letter this night, tis dangerous to be spoken,
I have lockt the letter in my closet, these injuries
The King now beares, will be revenged home
Ther's part of a power already landed,
We must incline to the King, I will seeke him, and
Privily releeve him, goe you and maintaine talke
With the Duke, that my charity be not of him
Perceived, if hee aske for me, I am ill, and gon
To bed, though I die for't, as no lesse is threatned me,
The King my old master must be releeved, there is
Some strange thing toward, *Edmund* pray you be carefull. *Exit.*
  Bast. This curtesie forbid thee, shal the Duke instanly
And of that letter to, this seems a faire deserving (know
And must draw me that which my father looses, no lesse
Then all, then yonger rises when the old doe fall.   *Exit.*

Enter Lear, Kent, and foole.

  Kent. Here is the place my Lord, good my Lord enter, the
tyrannie of the open nights too ruffe for nature to indure.
  Lear. Let me alone.   *Kent.* Good my Lord enter.
  Lear. Wilt breake my heart?
  Kent. I had rather breake mine owne, good my Lord enter.
  Lear. Thou think'st tis much, that this tempestious storme
Invades us to the skin, so tis to thee,
But where the greater malady is fixt
The lesser is scarce felt, thoud'st shun a Beare,
But if thy flight lay toward the roring sea,
Thoud'st meet the beare it'h mouth, when the mind's free
The bodies delicate, this tempest in my mind
Doth from my sences take all feeling else

[114]

Save what beates their filiall ingratitude,
Is it not as this mouth should teare this hand
For lifting food to't, but I will punish sure,
No I will weepe no more, in such a night as this!
O *Regan*, *Gonorill*, your old kind father   (lies,
Whose franke heart gave you all, O that way madnes
Let me shun that, no more of that.

   Kent. Good my Lord enter.

   Lear. Prethe goe in thy selfe, seeke thy one ease
This tempest will not give me leave to ponder
On things would hurt me more, but ile goe in,
Poore naked wretches, where so ere you are
That bide the pelting of this pittiles night,
How shall your house-lesse heads, and unfed sides,
Your loopt and windowed raggednes defend you
From seasons such as these, O I have tane
Too little care of this, take physicke pompe,
Expose thy selfe to feele what wretches feele,
That thou mayst shake the superflux to them,
And shew the heavens more just.

   Foole. Come not in here Nunckle, her's a spirit, helpe me,
helpe mee.

   Kent. Give me thy hand, whose there.

   Foole. A spirit, he sayes, his nam's poore *Tom*.

   Kent. What art thou that dost grumble there in the straw,
come forth?

   Edg. Away, the fowle fiend followes me, thorough the
sharpe hathorne blowes the cold wind, goe to thy cold bed
and warme thee.

   Lear. Hast thou given all to thy two daughters, and art
thou come to this?

   Edg. Who gives anything to poore *Tom*, whome the foule
Fiende hath led, through fire, and through foord, and whirli-
poole, ore bog and quagmire, that has layd knives under his
pillow, and halters in his pue, set ratsbane by his pottage,
made him proud of heart, to ride on a bay trotting horse over
foure incht bridges, to course his owne shadow for a traytor,

[115]

blesse thy five wits, *Toms* a cold, blesse thee from whirle-winds, starreblusting, and taking, doe poore *Tom* some charitie, whom the foule fiend vexes, there could I have him now, and there, and and there againe.

Lear. What, his daughters brought him to this passe,
Couldst thou save nothing, didst thou give them all?

Foole. Nay he reserv'd a blanket, else we had beene all sham'd.

Lear. Now all the plagues that in the pendulous ayre
Hang fated ore mens faults, fall on thy daughters.

Kent. He hath no daughters sir.

Lear. Death traytor, nothing could have subdued nature
To such a lownes, but his unkind daughters,
Is it the fashion that discarded fathers,
Should have thus little mercy on their flesh,
Judicious punishment twas this flesh
Begot those Pelicane daughters.

Edg. Pilicock sate on pelicocks hill, a lo lo lo.

Foole. This cold night will turne us all to fooles & madmen.

Edg. Take heede at'h foule fiend, obay thy parents, keep thy words justly, sweare not, commit not with mans sworne spouse, set not thy sweet heart on proud array, *Toms* a cold.

Lear. What hast thou beene?

Edg. A Servingman, proud in heart and mind, that curld my haire, wore gloves in my cap, served the lust of my mistris heart, and did the act of darkenes with her, swore as many oaths as I spake words, and broke them in the sweet face of heaven, one that slept in the contriving of lust, and wakt to doe it, wine loved I deeply, dice deerely, and in woman out paromord the Turke, false of heart, light of eare, bloudie of hand, Hog in sloth, Fox in stealth, Woolfe in greedines,, Dog in madnes, Lyon in pray, let not the creeking of shooes, nor the ruslngs of silkes betray thy poore heart to women, keepe thy foote out of brothell, thy hand out of placket, thy pen from lenders booke, and defie the foule fiend, still through the hathorne blowes the cold wind, hay no on ny, Dolphin my boy, my boy, caese let him trot by.

Lear. Why thou wert better in thy grave, then to answere with thy uncovered bodie this extremitie of the skies, is man no more, but this consider him well, thou owest the worme no silke, the beast no hide, the sheepe no wooll, the cat no perfume, her's three ons are so phisticated, thou art the thing it selfe, unaccomodated man, is no more but such a poore bare forked Animall as thou art, off off you lendings, come on

Foole. Prithe Nunckle be content, this is a naughty night to swim in, now a little fire in a wild field, were like an old leachers heart, a small sparke, all the rest in bodie cold, looke here comes a walking fire.   *Enter Gloster.*

Edg. This is the foule fiend *fliberdegibek*, hee begins at curphew, and walks till the first cocke, he gives the web, & the pin, squemes the eye, and makes the hare lip, mildewes the white wheate, and hurts the poore creature of earth, swithald footed thrice the old, he met the night mare and her nine fold bid her, O light and her troth plight and arint thee, witch arint thee.

Kent. How fares your Grace?

Lear. Whats hee?

Kent. Whose there, what i'st you seeke?

Glost. What are you there? your names?

Edg. Poore *Tom*, that eats the swimming frog, the tode, the todpole, the wall-newt, and the water, that in the furie of his heart, when the foule fiend rages, eats cow-dung for sallets, swallowes the old ratt, and the ditch dogge, drinkes the greene mantle of the standing poole, who is whipt from tithing to tithing, and stock-punisht and imprisoned, who hath had three sutes to his backe, sixe shirts to his bodie, horse to ride, and weapon to weare.

But mise and rats, and such small Deere,

Hath beene *Toms* foode for seven long yeare

Beware my follower, peace snulbug, peace thou fiend.

Glost. What hath your Grace no better company?

Edg. The Prince of darkenes is a Gentleman, *modo* he's caled and ma hu———

[117]

Glost. Our flesh and bloud is growne so vild my Lord, that it doth hate what gets it.

Edg. Poore *Toms* a cold.

Glost. Go in with me, my dutie cannot suffer to obay in all your daughters hard commaunds, though their injunction be to barre my doores, and let this tyranous night take hold upon you, yet have I venter'd to come seeke you out, and bring you where both food and fire is readie.

Lear. First let me talke with this Philosopher,
What is the cause of thunder?

Kent. My good Lord take his offer, goe into the house.

Lear. Ile talke a word with this most learned Theban, what is your studie?

Edg. How to prevent the fiend, and to kill vermine.

Lear. Let me aske you one word in private.

Kent. Importune him to goe my Lord, his wits begin

Glost. Canst thou blame him,   (to unsettle,
His daughters seeke his death, O that good *Kent*,
He said it would be thus, poore banisht man,
Thou sayest the King growes mad, ile tell thee friend
I am almost mad my selfe, I had a sonne
Now out-lawed from my bloud, a sought my life
But lately, very late, I lov'd him friend
No father his sonne deerer, true to tell thee,
The greefe hath craz'd my wits,
What a nights this? I doe beseech your Grace.

Lear. O crie you mercie noble Philosopher, your com-

Edg. *Toms* a cold.   (pany.

Glost. In fellow there, in't hovell keepe thee warme.

Lear. Come lets in all.

Kent. This way my Lord.

Lear. With him, I wil keep stil, with my Philosopher.

Ken. Good my Lord sooth him, let him take the fellow.

Glost. Take him you on.

Kent. Sirah come on, goe along with us?

Lear. Come good Athenian.

Glost. No words, no words, hush.

Edg. Child *Rowland*, to the darke towne come,
His word was still fy fo and fum,
I smell the bloud of a British man.

Enter Cornewell and Bastard.

Corn. I will have my revenge ere I depart the house.
Bast. How my Lord I may be censured, that nature thus gives way to loyaltie, some thing feares me to thinke of.
Corn. I now perceive it was not altogether your brothers evill disposition made him seeke his death, but a provoking merit, set a worke by a reproveable badnes in himselfe.
Bast. How malicious is my fortune, that I must repent to bee just? this is the letter he spoke of, which approves him an intelligent partie to the advantages of *France*, O heavens that his treason were, or not I the detecter.
Corn. Goe with me to the Dutches.
Bast. If the matter of this paper be certaine, you have mighty busines in hand.
Corn. True or false, it hath made thee Earle of *Gloster*, seeke out where thy father is, that hee may bee readie for our apprehension.
Bast. If I find him comforting the King, it will stuffe his suspition more fully, I will persevere in my course of loyaltie, though the conflict be sore betweene that and my bloud.
Corn. I will lay trust upon thee, and thou shalt find a dearer father in my love.   *Exit.*

Enter Gloster and Lear, Kent, Foole, and Tom.

Glost. Here is better then the open ayre, take it thankfully, I will peece out the comfort with what addition I can, I will not be long from you.
Ken. All the power of his wits have given way to impatience, the Gods deserve your kindnes.
Edg. *Fretereto* cals me, and tels me *Nero* is an angler in the lake of darknes, pray innocent beware the foule fiend.

[119]

Foole. Prithe Nunckle tell me, whether a madman be a Gentleman or a Yeoman.

Lear. A King, a King, to have a thousand with red burning spits come hiszing in upon them.

Edg. The foule fiend bites my backe,

Foole. He's mad, that trusts the tamenes of a Wolfe, a horses health, a boyes love, or a whores oath.

Lear. It shalbe done, I will arraigne them straight,
Come sit thou here most learned Justice
Thou sapient sir sit here, no you shee Foxes––

Edg. Looke where he stands and glars, wanst thou eyes, at tral madam come ore the broome*Bessy* to mee.

Foole. Her boat hath a leake, and she must not speake,
Why she dares not come, over to thee.

Edg. The foule fiend haunts poore *Tom* in the voyce of a nigh Hoppedance cries in *Toms* belly for two white herring, (tingale, Croke not blacke Angell, I have no foode for thee.

Kent. How doe you sir? stand you not so amazd, will you lie downe and rest upon the cushings?

Lear. Ile see their triall first, bring in their evidence, thou robbed man of Justice take thy place, & thou his yokefellow of equity, bench by his side, you are ot'h commission, sit you too.

Ed. Let us deale justly sleepest or wakest thou jolly shepheard, Thy sheepe bee in the corne, and for one blast of thy minikin mouth, thy sheepe shall take no harme, Pur the cat is gray.

Lear. Arraigne her first tis *Gonoril*, I here take my oath before this honorable assembly kickt the poore king her father.

Foole. Come hither mistrisse is your name *Gonorill*.

Lear. She cannot deny it.

Fool. Cry you mercy I tooke you for a joyne stoole.

Lear. And heres another whose warpt lookes proclaime,
What store her hart is made an, stop her there,
Armes, armes, sword, fire, corruption in the place,
False Justicer why hast thou let her scape.

Edg. Blesse thy five wits.

Kent. O pity sir, where is the patience now,
That you so oft have boasted to retaine.

Edg. My teares begin to take his part so much,
Theile marre my counterfeiting.

Lear. The little dogs and all
Trey, Blanch, and Sweet hart, see they barke at me.

Edg. *Tom* will throw his head at them, avant you curs,
Be thy mouth, or blacke, or white, tooth that poysons if it bite,
Mastife, grayhound, mungril, grim-houd or spaniel, brach or him,
Bobtaile tike, or trundletaile, Tom will make them weep and waile,
For with throwing thus my head, dogs leape the hatch and all
are fled, loudla doodla come march to wakes, and faires, and
market townes, poore *Tom* thy horne is dry.   (her

Lear. Then let them anotomize *Regan*, see what breeds about
Hart is there any cause in nature that makes this hardnes,
You sir, I entertaine you for one of my hundred,
Only I do not like the fashion of your garments youle say,
They are Persian attire, but let them be chang'd.

Kent. Now good my Lord lie here awhile.

Lear. Make no noise, make no noise, draw the cutains, so,
so, so,
Weele go to supper it'h morning, so, so, so,   *Enter Gloster.*

Glost. Come hither friend, where is the King my maister.

Kent. Here sir, but trouble him not his wits are gon.

Glost. Good friend I prithy take him in thy armes,
I have or'e heard a plot of death upon him,
Ther is a Litter ready lay him in't, & drive towards Dover frend,
Where thou shalt meet both welcome & protection, take up thy
If thou shoud'st dally halfe an houre, his life with thine (master
And all that offer to defend him stand in assured losse,
Take up the King and followe me, that will to some provision
Give thee quick conduct.

Kent. Oppressed nature sleepes,
This rest might yet have balmed thy broken sinewes,
Which if convenience will not alow stand in hard cure,
Come helpe to beare thy maister, thou must not stay behind.

Glost. Come, come away.   *Exit.*

[121]

Edg. When we our betters see bearing our woes: we scarcely
thinke, our miseries, our foes.
Who alone suffers suffers, most it'h mind,
Leaving free things and happy showes behind,
But then the mind much sufferance doth or'e scip,
When griefe hath mates, and bearing fellowship:
How light and portable my paine seemes now,
When that which makes me bend, makes the King bow.
He childed as I fathered, *Tom* away,
Marke the high noyses and thy selfe bewray,
When false opinion whose wrong thoughts defile thee,
In thy just proofe repeals and reconciles thee,
What will hap more to night, safe scape the King,
Lurke, lurke.

    Enter Cornwall, and Regan, and Gonorill, and Bastard.

                                     (letter

    Corn. Post speedily to my Lord your husband shew him this
The army of France is landed, seeke out the vilaine *Gloster*.
    Regan. Hang him instantly.
    Gon. Plucke out his eyes.
    Corn. Leave him to my displeasure, *Edmund* keep you our
                                   (sister company.
The revenge we are bound to take upon your trayterous father,
Are not fit for your beholding, advise the Duke where you are
To a most festuant preparation we are bound to the like, (going
Our past shall be swift and intelligence betwixt us,
Farewell deere sister, farewell my Lord of *Gloster*,
How now whers the King?   *Enter Steward.*
    Stew. My Lord of *Gloster* hath conveyd him hence,
Some five or sixe and thirtie of his Knights hot questrits after
him, met him at gate, who with some other of the Lords
dependants are gone with him towards Dover, where they
boast to have well armed friends.
    Corn. Get horses for you mistris.
    Gon. Farewell sweet Lord and sister. *Exit Gon. and Bast.*
    Corn. Edmund farewell. goe seeke the traytor *Gloster*.

Pinion him like a theefe, bring him before us,
Though we may not passe upon his life
Without the forme of Justice, yet our power
Shall doe a curtesie to our wrath, which men may blame
But not controule, whose there, the traytor?

Enter Gloster brought in by two or three,

Reg. Ingratfull Fox tis hee.
Corn. Bind fast his corkie armes.
Glost. What meanes your Graces, good my friends consider,
You are my gests, doe me no foule play friends.
Corn. Bind him I say,
Reg. Hard hard, O filthie traytor!
Glost. Unmercifull Lady as you are, I am true.
Corn. To this chaire bind him, villaine thou shalt find———
Glost. By the kind Gods tis most ignobly done, to pluck
me by the beard.   *Reg.* So white and such a Traytor.
Glost. Naughty Ladie, these haires which thou dost ravish
Will quicken and accuse thee, I am your host. (from my chin
With robbers hands my hospitable favours
You should not ruffell thus, what will you doe.
Corn. Come sir, what letters had you late from *France*?
Reg. Be simple answerer, for we know the truth.
Corn. And what confederacy have you with the tratours
late footed in the kingdome?
Reg. To whose hands you have sent the lunatick King
speake?
Glost. I have a letter gessingly set downe
Which came from one, that's of a neutrall heart,
And not from one oppos'd.
Corn. Cunning.   *Reg.* And false.
Corn. Where hast thou sent the King?   *Glost.* To Dover.
Reg. Wherefore to Dover? wast thou not charg'd at perill——
Corn. Wherefore to Dover? let him first answere that.
Glost. I am tide tot'h stake, and I must stand the course.
Reg. Wherefore to Dover sir?
Glost. Because I would not see thy cruell nayles

[123]

Pluck out his poore old eyes, nor thy fierce sister
In his annoynted flesh rash borish phangs,
The Sea with such a storme on his lowd head
In hell blacke night indur'd, would have bod up
And quencht the stelled fires, yet poore old heart,
Hee holpt the heavens to rage,
If wolves had at thy gate heard that dearne time
Thou shouldst have said, good Porter turne the key,
All cruels else subscrib'd but I shall see
The winged vengeance overtake such children.

   Corn. Seet shalt thou never, fellowes hold the chaire,
Upon those eyes of thine, Ile set my foote.

   Glost. He that will thinke to live till he be old
Give me some helpe, O cruell, O ye Gods!

   Reg. One side will mocke another, tother to.

   Corn. If you see vengeance———

   Servant. Hold your hand my Lord
I have serv'd ever since I was a child   (you hold.
But better service have I never done you, then now to bid

   Reg. How now you dogge.

   Serv. If you did weare a beard upon your chin id'e shake it
on this quarrell, what doe you meane?

   Corn. My villaine.   *draw and fight.*

   Serv. Why then come on, and take the chance of anger.

   Reg. Give me thy sword, a pesant stand up thus.

      Shee takes a sword and runs at him behind.

   Servant. Oh I am slaine my Lord, yet have you only one
eye left to see some mischiefe on him, oh!

   Corn. Least it see more prevent it, out vild Jelly
Where is thy luster now?

   Glost. All darke and comfortles, wher's my sonne *Edmund?*
Edmund unbridle all the sparks of nature, to quit this horred act.

   Reg. Out villaine, thou calst on him that hates thee, it was
he that made the overture of thy treasons to us, who is too
good to pittie thee.

   Glost. O my follies, then *Edgar* was abus'd,

and His three Daughters

Kind Gods forgive me that, and prosper him.

Reg. Goe thrust him out at gates, and let him smell his way to Dover, how ist my Lord? how looke you?

Corn. I have receiv'd a hurt, follow me Ladie, Turne out that eyles villaine, throw his slave upon The dungell *Regan*, I bleed apace, untimely Comes this hurt, give me your arme.   *Exit.*

Servant. Ile never care what wickednes I doe, If this man come to good.

2 *Servant.* If she live long, & in the end meet the old course of death, women will all turne monsters.

1 *Ser.* Lets follow the old Earle, and get the bedlom To lead him where he would, his madnes Allows it selfe to any thing.

2 *Ser.* Goe thou, ile fetch some flaxe and whites of egges to apply to his bleeding face, now heaven helpe him. *Exit.*

Enter Edgar.

Edg. Yet better thus, and knowne to be contemnd, Then still contemn'd and flattered to be worst, The lowest and most dejected thing of Fortune Stands still in experience, lives not in feare, The lamentable change is from the best, The worst returnes to laughter, Who's here, my father parti, eyd, world, world, O world! But that thy strange mutations make us hate thee, Life would not yeeld to age. *Enter Glost. led by an old man.*

Old man. O my good Lord, I have beene your tenant, & your fathers tenant this forescore———

Glost. Away, get thee away, good friend be gon, Thy comforts can doe me no good at all, Thee they may hurt.

Old man. Alack sir, you cannot see your way.

Glost. I have no way, and therefore want no eyes, I stumbled when I saw, full oft tis seene Our meanes secure us, and our meare defects Prove our comodities, ah deere sonne *Edgar,*

[125]

The food of thy abused fathers wrath,
Might I but live to see thee in my tuch,
Id'e say I had eyes againe.

    Old man. How now whose there?

    Edg. O Gods, who ist can say I am at the worst,
I am worse then ere I was.

    Old man. Tis poore mad *Tom.*

    Edg. And worse I may be yet, the worst is not,
As long as we can say, this is the worst.

    Old man. Fellow where goest?

    Glost. Is it a begger man?

    Old man. Mad man, and begger to.

    Glost. A has some reason, else he could not beg,
In the last nights storme I such a fellow saw,
Which made me thinke a man a worme, my sonne
Came then into my mind, and yet my mind   (since,
Was then scarce friendes with him, I have heard more
As flies are toth' wanton boyes, are we toth' Gods,
They bitt us for their sport.

    Edg. How should this be, bad is the trade that must play
the foole to sorrow angring it selfe and others, blesse thee
maister.

    Glost. Is that the naked fellow?

    Old man. I my Lord.

    Glost. Then prethee get thee gon, if for my sake
Thou wilt oretake us here a mile or twaine
Ith' way toward Dover, doe it for ancient love
And bring some covering for this naked soule
Who Ile intreate to leade me.

    Old man. Alack sir he is mad.

    Glost. Tis the times plague, when madmen lead the
Doe as I bid thee, or rather doe thy pleasure,   (blind,
Above the rest, be gon.

    Old man. Ile bring him the best parrell that I have
Come on't what will.

    Glost. Sirrah naked fellow.

    Edg. Poore *Toms* a cold, I cannot dance it farther.

Glost. Come hither fellow.

Edg. Blesse thy sweete eyes, they bleed.

Glost. Knowst thou the way to Dover?

Edg. Both stile and gate, horse way, and foot-path,
Poore *Tom* hath beene scard out of his good wits,
Blesse the good man from the foule fiend,
Five fiends have beene in poore *Tom* at once,
Of lust, as *Obidicut*, *Hobbididence* Prince of dumbnes,
Mahu of stealing, *Modo* of murder, *Stiberdigebit* of
Mobing, & *Mobing* who since possesses chambermaids
And waiting women, so, blesse thee maister.   (plagues.

Glost. Here take this purse, thou whome the heavens
Have humbled to all strokes, that I am wretched, makes
The happier, heavens deale so still,   (thee
Let the superfluous and lust-dieted man
That stands your ordinance, that will not see
Because he does not feele, feele your power quickly,
So distribution should under excesse,
And each man have enough, dost thou know Dover?

Edg. I master.

Glost. There is a cliffe whose high & bending head
Lookes firmely in the confined deepe,
Bring me but to the very brimme of it
And ile repaire the misery thou dost beare
With something rich about me,
From that place I shal no leading need.

Edg. Give me thy arme, poore *Tom* shall lead thee.

Enter Gonorill and Bastard.

Gon. Welcome my Lord, I marvaile our mild husband
Not met us on the way, now wher's your maister?

Enter Steward.

Stew. Madame within, but never man so chang'd, I told
him of the army that was landed, he smild at it, I told
you were coming, his answere was the worse, of *Glosters*
treacherie, and of the loyall service of his sonne when I
enform'd him, then hee cald me sott, and told me I had turnd

the wrong side out, what hee should most desire seemes
pleasant to him, what like offensive.

  Gon. Then shall you goe no further,
It is the cowish terrer of his spirit
That dares not undermake, hele not feele wrongs
Which tie him to an answere, our wishes on the way
May prove effects, backe *Edgar* to my brother,
Hasten his musters, and conduct his powers
I must change armes at home, and give the distaffe
Into my husbands hands, this trusty servant
Shall passe betweene us, ere long you are like to heare
If you dare venture in your owne behalfe
A mistresses command, weare this, spare speech,
Decline your head: this kisse if it durst speake
Would stretch thy spirits up into the ayre,
Conceave and far you well.

  Bast. Yours in the ranks of death.   (are dew

  Gon. My most deer *Gloster*, to thee a womans services
A foole usurps my bed.

  Stew. Madam here comes my Lord.   *Exit Stew.*

  Gon. I have beene worth the whistling.   (rude wind

  Alb. O *Gonoril*, you are not worth the dust which the
Blowes in your face, I feare your disposition
That nature which contemnes ith origin
Cannot be bordered certaine in it selfe,
She that her selfe will sliver and disbranch
From her materiall sap, perforce must wither,
And come to deadly use.

  Gon. No more, the text is foolish.

  Alb. Wisedome and goodnes, to the vild seeme vild,
Filths favor but themselves, what have you done?
Tigers, not daughters, what have you perform'd?
A father, and a gracious aged man
Whose reverence even the head-lugd beare would lick.
Most barbarous, most degenerate have you madded,
Could my good brother suffer you to doe it?
A man, a Prince, by him so benifited,

If that the heavens doe not their visible spirits (come
Send quickly downe to tame this vild offences, it will
Humanity must perforce pray on it self like monsters of
   Gon. Milke liverd man   (the deepe.
That barest a cheeke for bloes, a head for wrongs,
Who hast not in thy browes an eye deserving thine honour,
From thy suffering, that not know'st, fools do those vilains pitty
Who are punisht ere they have done their mischiefe,
Wher's thy drum? *France* spreds his banners in our noyseles land,
With plumed helme, thy state begins thereat
Whil'st thou a morall foole sits still and cries
Alack why does he so?
   Alb. See thy selfe devill, proper deformity shewes not in
the fiend, so horrid as in woman.
   Gon. O vaine foole!
   Alb. Thou changed, and selfe-coverd thing for shame
Be-monster not thy feature, wer't my fitnes
To let these hands obay my bloud,
They are apt enough to dislecate and teare
Thy flesh and bones, how ere thou art a fiend,
A womans shape doth shield thee.
   Gon. Marry your manhood mew———
   Alb. What news.   *Enter a Gentleman.*
   Gent. O my good Lord the Duke of *Cornwals* dead, slaine
by his servant, going to put out the other eye of *Gloster.*
   Alb. *Glosters* eyes?
   Gen. A servant that he bred, thrald with remorse,
Oppos'd against the act, bending his sword
To his great maister, who thereat inraged
Flew on him, and amongst them, feld him dead,
But not without that harmefull stroke, which since
Hath pluckt him after.
   Alb. This shewes you are above Justisers,
That these our nether crimes so speedely can venge.
But O poore *Gloster* lost he his other eye.   (answer,
   Gent. Both, both my Lord, this letter Madam craves a speedy
Tis from your sister.   *Gon.* One way I like this well,

[129]

But being widow and my *Gloster* with her,
May all the building on my fancie plucke,
Upon my hatefull life, another way the newes is not so tooke,
Ile read and answer.   *Exit.*

   Alb. Where was his sonne when they did take his eyes.
   Gent. Come with my Lady hither.   *Alb.* He is not here.
   Gent. No my good Lord I met him backe againe.
   Alb. Knowes he the wickednesse.
   Gent. I my good Lord twas he informd against him,
And quit the house on purpose that there punishment
Might have the freer course.   (the King,
   Alb. Gloster I live to thanke thee for the love thou shewedst
And to revenge thy eyes, come hither friend,
Tell me what more thou knowest.   *Exit.*

Enter Kent and a Gentleman.

   Kent. Why the King of *Fraunce* is so suddenly gone backe,
know you no reason.
   Gent. Something he left imperfect in the state, which since his
comming forth is thought of, which imports to the Kingdome,
So much feare and danger that his personall returne was most
required and necessarie.
   Kent. Who hath he left behind him, General.
   Gent. The Marshall of *France* Monsier *la Far.*   (of griefe.
   Kent. Did your letters pierce the queene to any demonstration
   Gent. I say she tooke them, read them in my presence,
And now and then an ample teare trild downe
Her delicate cheeke, it seemed she was a queene over her passion,
Who most rebell-like, fought to be King ore her.
   Kent. O then it moved her.
   Gent. Not to a rage, patience and sorow streme,
Who should expresse her goodliest you have seene,
Sun shine and raine at once, her smiles and teares,
Were like a better way those happie smilets,
That playd on her ripe lip seeme not to know,
What guests were in her eyes which parted thence,
As pearles from diamonds dropt in briefe,

Sorow would be a raritie most beloved,
If all could so become it.
   Kent. Made she no verball question.
   Gent. Faith once or twice she heav'd the name of father,
Pantingly forth as if it prest her heart,
Cried sisters, sisters, shame of Ladies sisters:
Kent, father, sisters, what ith storme ith night,
Let pitie not be beleeft there she shooke,
The holy water from her heavenly eyes,
And clamour moystened her, then away she started,
To deale with griefe alone.
   Kent. It is the stars, the stars above us governe our conditions,
Else one selfe mate and make could not beget,
Such different issues, you spoke not with her since.
   Gent. No.   *Kent.* Was this before the King returnd.
   Gent. No, since.
   Kent. Well sir, the poore distressed *Lears* ith towne,
Who some time in his better tune remembers,
What we are come about, and by no meanes will yeeld to see his
   Gent. Why good sir?   (daughter.
   Kent. A soveraigne shame so elbows him his own unkindnes
That stript her from his benediction turnd her,
To forraine casualties gave her deare rights,
To his dog-harted daughters, these things sting his mind,
So venomously that burning shame detaines him from *Cordelia.*
   Gent. Alack poore Gentleman.
   Kent. Of *Albanies* and *Cornewals* powers you heard not.
   Gent. Tis so they are a foote.
   Kent. Well sir, ile bring you to our maister *Lear,*
And leave you to attend him some deere cause,
Will in concealement wrap me up awhile,
When I am knowne aright you shall not greeve,
Lending me this acquaintance, I pray you go along with me.
                                        Exit

       Enter Cordelia, Doctor and others.

   Cor. Alack tis he, why he was met even now,

As mad as the vent sea singing aloud,
Crownd with ranke femiter and furrow weedes,
With hor-docks, hemlocke, netles, cookow flowers,
Darnell and all the idle weedes that grow,
In our sustayning, corne, a centurie is sent forth,
Search every acre in the hie growne field,
And bring him to our eye, what can mans wisdome
In the restoring his bereved sence, he that can helpe him
Take all my outward worth.
    Doct. There is meanes Madame.
Our foster nurse of nature is repose,
The which he lackes that to provoke in him,
And many simples operative whose power,
Will close the eye of anguish.
    Cord. All blest secrets all you unpublisht vertues of the earth,
Spring with my teares be aydant and remediat,
In the good mans distresse, seeke, seeke, for him,
Lest his ungovernd rage dissolve the life.
That wants the meanes to lead it.   *Enter messenger.*
    Mes. News Madam, the Brittish powers are marching hither-
    Cord. Tis knowne before, our preparation stands, (ward.
In expect action of them, ô deere father
It is thy busines that I go about, therfore great *France*
My mourning and important teares hath pitied,
No blowne ambition doth our armes in fight
But love, deere love, and our ag'd fathers right,
Soone may I heare and see him.   *Exit.*

Enter Regan and Steward.

    Reg. But are my brothers powers set forth?
    Stew. I Madam.   *Reg.* Himselfe in person?
    Stew. Madam with much ado, your sister is the better soldier.
    Reg. Lord *Edmund* spake not with your Lady at home.
    Stew. No Madam.
    Reg. What might import my sisters letters to him?
    Stew. I know not Lady.
    Reg. Faith he is posted hence on serious matter,

It was great ignorance, *Glosters* eyes being out
To let him live, where he arives he moves
All harts against us, and now I thinke is gone
In pitie of his misery to dispatch his nighted life,
Moreover to discrie the strength at'h army.

   Stew. I must needs after him with my letters

   Reg. Our troope sets forth to morrow stay with us,
The wayes are dangerous.

   Stew. I may not Madame, my Lady charg'd my dutie in
this busines.

   Reg. Why should she write to *Edmund?* might not you
Transport her purposes by word, belike
Some thing, I know not what, ile love thee much,
Let me unseale the letter.

   Stew. Madam I'de rather———

   Reg. I know your Lady does not love her husband
I am sure of that, and at her late being here
Shee gave strange aliads, and most speaking lookes
To noble *Edmund*, I know you are of her bosome.

   Stew. I Madam.

   Reg. I speake in understanding, for I know't,
Therefore I doe advise you take this note,
My Lord is dead, *Edmund* and I have talkt,
And more convenient is he for my hand
Then for your Ladies, you may gather more
If you doe find him, pray you give him this,
And when your mistris heares thus much from you
I pray desire her call her wisedome to her, so farewell,
If you doe chance to heare of that blind traytor,
Preferment fals on him that cuts him off.

   Ste. Would I could meet him Madam, I would shew
What Lady I doe follow.

   Reg. Fare thee well.   *Exit.*

      Enter Gloster and Edmund.

   Glost. When shall we come toth' top of that same hill?

[133]

Edg. You do climbe it up now, looke how we labour?

Glost. Me thinks the ground is even.

Edg. Horrible steepe, harke doe you heare the sea?

Glost. No truly.

Edg. Why then your other sences grow imperfect
By your eyes anguish.

Glost. So may it be indeed,
Me thinks thy voyce is altered, and thou speakest
With better phrase and matter then thou didst.

Edg. Y'ar much deceaved, in nothing am I chang'd
But in my garments.

Glost. Me thinks y'ar better spoken.   (feareful

Edg. Come on sir, her's the place, stand still, how
And dizi tis to cast ones eyes so low
The crowes and choghes that wing the midway ayre
Shew scarce so grosse as beetles, halfe way downe
Hangs one that gathers sampire, dreadfull trade,
Me thinkes he seemes no bigger then his head,
The fishermen that walke upon the beach
Appeare like mise, and yon tall anchoring barke
Diminisht to her cock, her cock a boui
Almost too small for sight, the murmuring surge
That on the unnumbred idle peeble chaffes
Cannot be heard, its so hie ile looke no more,
Least my braine turne, and the deficient sight
Topple downe headlong.

Glost. Set me where you stand?

Edg. Give me your hand, you are now within a foot
Of th'extreame verge, for all beneath the Moone
Would I not leape upright.

Glost. Let goe my hand,
Here friend's another pursse, in it a jewell,
Well worth a poore mans taking, Fairies and Gods
Prosper it with thee, goe thou farther off,
Bid me farewell, and let me heare thee going.

Edg. Now fare you well good sir.

Glost. With all my heart.   (to cure it.
Edg. Why I do trifell thus with his dispaire is done
  Glost. O you mightie Gods,   *He kneeles.*
This world I doe renounce, and in your sights
Shake patiently my great affliction off,
If I could beare it longer and not fall
To quarel with your great opposles wils
My snurff and loathed part of nature should
Burne it selfe out, if *Edgar* live, O blesse,
Now fellow fare thee well.   *He fals.*
  Edg. Gon sir, farewell, and yet I know not how conceit
my robbe the treasurie of life, when life it selfe yealds to the
thefe, had he beene where he thought by this had thought
beene past, alive or dead, ho you sir, heare you sir, speak,
thus might he passe indeed, yet he revives, what are you sir?
  Glost. Away and let me die.
  Edg. Hadst thou beene ought but gosmore feathers ayre,
So many fadome downe precipitating
Thou hadst shiverd like an egge, but thou dost breath
Hast heavy substance, bleedst not, speakest, art found,
Ten masts at each make not the altitude,
Which thou hast perpendicularly fell,
Thy lifes a miracle, speake yet againe.
  Glost. But have I fallen or no I.
  Edg. From the dread sommons of this chalkie borne,
Looke up a hight, the shrill gorg'd larke so farre
Cannot bee seene or heard, doe but looke up?
  Glost. Alack I have no eyes
Is wretchednes depriv'd, that benefit
To end it selfe by death twas yet some comfort
When misery could beguile the tyrants rage
And frustrate his proud will.
  Edg. Give me your arme?
Up, so, how feele you your legges, you stand.
  Glost. Too well, too well.
  Edg. This is above all strangenes
Upon the crowne of the cliffe what thing was that

Which parted from you.

    Glost. A poore unfortunate bagger.

    Edg. As I stood here below me thoughts his eyes
Were two full Moones, a had a thousand noses
Hornes, welk't and waved like the enridged sea,
It was some fiend, therefore thou happy father
Thinke that the cleerest Gods, who made their honours
Of mens impossibilities, have preserved thee.

    Glost. I doe remember now, henceforth ile beare
Affliction till it doe crie out it selfe
Enough, enough and die that thing you speake of,
I tooke it for a man, often would it say
The fiend the fiend, he led me to that place

    Edg. Bare free & patient thoughts, but who comes here
The safer sence will neare accommodate his maister thus.

Enter Lear mad.

    Lear. No they cannot touch mee for coyning, I am the king
    Edg. O thou side pearcing sight.   (himselfe.

    Lear. Nature is above Art in that respect, ther's your presse
money, that fellow handles his bow like a crow-keeper, draw
me a clothiers yard, looke, looke a mowse, peace, peace, this
tosted cheese will do it, ther's my gauntlet, ile prove it on a
gyant, bring up the browne-billes, O well flowne bird in the
ayre, hagh, give the word?   *Edg.* Sweet Margerum.

    Lear. Passe.   *Glost.* I know that voyce.

    Lear. Ha *Gonorill,* ha *Regan,* they flattered mee like a
dogge, and tould me I had white haires in my beard, ere the
black ones were there, to say I and no, to every thing I saide,
I and no toe, was no good divinitie, when the raine came to
wet me once, and the winde to make mee chatter, when the
thunder would not peace at my bidding, there I found them,
there I smelt them out, goe toe, they are not men of their
words, they told mee I was every thing, tis a lye, I am not
argue-proofe.

    Glost. The tricke of the voyce I doe well remember, ist
not the King?

[136]

Lear. I ever inch a King when I do stare, see how the subject quakes, I pardon that mans life, what was thy cause, adultery? thou shalt not die for adulterie, no the wren goes toot, and the smal guilded flie doe letcher in my sight, let copulation thrive, for *Glosters* bastard son was kinder to his father then my daughters got tweene the lawfull sheets, toot luxurie, *pell, mell*, for I lacke souldiers, behold yon simpring dame whose face between her forkes presageth snow, that minces vertue, and do shake the head heare of pleasures name to fichew nor the foyled horse goes toot with a more riotous appetite, down from the wast tha're centaures, though women all above, but to the girdle doe the gods inherit, beneath is all the fiends, thers hell, thers darknesse, ther's the sulphury pit, burning, scalding, stench, consumation, fie, fie, fie, pah, pah, Give mee an ounce of Civet, good Apothocarie, to sweeten my imagination, ther's money for thee.

Glost. O let me kisse that hand.

Lear. Here wipe it first, it smels of mortalitie.

Glost. O ruind peece of nature, this great world should so weare out to naught, do you know me?

Lear. I remember thy eyes well inough, dost thou squiny on me, no do thy worst blind *Cupid*, ile not love, reade thou that challenge, marke the penning oft.

Glost. Were all the letters sunnes I could not see one.

Edg. I would not take this from report, it is, and my heart breakes at it. *Lear.* Read. *Glost.* What! with the case of eyes

Lear. O ho, are you there with me, no eyes in your head, nor no mony in your purse, your eyes are in a heavie case, your purse in a light, yet you see how this world goes.

Glost. I see it feelingly.

Lear. What art mad, a man may see how the world goes with no eyes, looke with thy eares, see how yon Justice railes upon yon simple theefe, harke in thy eare handy, dandy, which is the theefe, which is the Justice, thou hast seene a farmers dogge barke at a begger. *Glost.* I sir.

Lear. And the creature runne from the cur, there thou mightst behold the great image of authoritie, a dogge, so

[137]

bade in office, thou rascall beadle hold thy bloudy hand, why dost thou lash that whore, strip thine owne backe, thy bloud hotly lusts to use her in that kind for which thou whipst her, the usurer hangs the cosiner, through tottered raggs, smal vices do appeare, robes & furd-gownes hides all, get thee glasse eyes, and like a scurvy polititian seeme to see the things thou doest not, no now pull off my bootes, harder, harder, so.

Edg. O matter and impertinencie mixt reason in madnesse.

Lear. If thou wilt weepe my fortune take my eyes, I knowe thee well inough thy name is *Gloster*, thou must be patient, we came crying hither, thou knowest the first time that we smell the aire, we wayl and cry, I will preach to thee marke me.

Glost. Alack alack the day.

Lear. When we are borne, we crie that wee are come to this great stage of fooles, this a good blocke. It were a delicate stratagem to shoot a troupe of horse with fell, & when I have stole upon these sonne in lawes, then kill, kill, kill, kill, kill, kill.

Enter three Gentlemen.

Gent. O here he is, lay hands upon him sirs, your most deere

Lear. No reskue, what a prisoner, I am eene the naturall foole of Fortune, use me well you shall have ransome, let mee have a churgion I am cut to the braines.

Gent. You shall have any thing.

Lear. No seconds, all my selfe, why this would make a man of salt to use his eyes for garden waterpots, I and laying Autums dust.

Lear. I will die bravely like a bridegroome, what? I will be Joviall, come, come, I am a King my maisters, know you that.

Gent. You are a royall one, and we obey you.

Lear. Then theres life int, nay and you get it you shall get it with running.   *Exit King running.*

Gent. A sight most pitifull in the meanest wretch, past

speaking of in a king: thou hast one daughter who redeemes
nature from the generall curse which twaine hath brought her
to.

   Edg. Haile gentle sir.

   Gent. Sir speed you, whats your will.

   Edg. Do you heare ought of a battell toward.

   Gent. Most sure and vulgar every one here's that
That can distinguish sence.

   Edg. But by your favour how neers the other army.

   Gent. Neere and on speed fort the maine descryes,
Standst on the howerly thoughts.

   Edg. I thanke you sir thats all.

   Gent. Though that the Queene on speciall cause is here,
Hir army is moved on.   *Edg.* I thanke you sir.   *Exit.*

   Glost. You ever gentle gods take my breath from me,
Let not my worser spirit tempt me againe,
To dye before you please.   *Edg.* Well, pray you father.

   Glost. Now good sir what are you.

   Edg. A most poore man made lame by Fortunes blowes,
Who by the Art of knowne and feeling sorrowes
Am pregnant to good pitty, give me your hand
Ile lead you to some biding.

   Glost. Hartie thankes, the bounty and the benizon of
heaven, to boot, to boot.   *Enter Steward.*

   Stew. A proclamed prize, most happy, that eyles head of
thine was first framed flesh to rayse my fortunes, thou most
unhappy traytor, briefly thy selfe remember, the sword is
out that must destroy thee.

   Glost. Now let thy friendly hand put strength enough to't.

   Stew. Wherefore bould pesant durst thou support a
publisht traytor, hence least the infection of his fortune take
like hold on thee, let goe his arme?

   Edg. Chill not let goe sir without cagion.

   Stew. Let goe slave, or thou diest.

   Edg. Good Gentleman goe your gate, let poore voke
passe, and chud have beene swaggar'd out of my life, it
would not have beene so long by vortnight, nay come not

neare the old man, keepe out chevore ye, ore ile trie whether
your costerd or my bat be the harder, ile be plaine with you.
 Stew. Out dunghill.   *they fight.*
 Edg. Chill pick your teeth sir, come, no matter for your foyns.
 Stew. Slave thou hast slaine me, villaine take my pursse,
If ever thou wilt thrive, burie my bodie,
And give the letters which thou find'st about me
To *Edmund* Earle of *Gloster*, seeke him out, upon
The *Brittish* partie, ô untimely death! death.   *He dies.*
 Edg. I know thee well, a serviceable villaine,
As dutious to the vices of thy mistris, as badnes would
 Glost. What is he dead?   (desire.
 Edg. Sit you down father, rest you, lets see his pockets
These letters that he speakes of, may be my friends,
Hee's dead, I am only sorrow he had no other deathsman
Let us see, leave gentle waxe, and manners blame us not
To know our enemies minds, wee'd rip their hearts,
Their papers is more lawfull.   *A letter.*

 Let your reciprocall vowes bee remembred, you have
many opportunities to cut him off, if your will want not,
time and place will be fruitfully offered, there is nothing
done, If he returne the conquerour, then am I the prisoner,
and his bed my jayle, from the lothed warmth whereof
deliver me, and supply the place for your labour, your wife
(so I would say) your affectionate servant and for you her
owne for *Venter, Gonorill.*

 Edg. O Indistinguisht space of womans wit,
A plot upon her vertuous husbands life,
And the exchange my brother heere in the sands,
Thee ile rake up, the post unsanctified
Of murtherous leachers, and in the mature time,
With this ungratious paper strike the sight
Of the death practis'd Duke, for him tis well,
That of thy death and businesse I can tell.
 Glost. The King is mad, how stiffe is my vild sence,
That I stand up and have ingenious feeling
Of my huge sorowes, better I were distract,

[140]

So should my thoughts be fenced from my griefes,
And woes by wrong imaginations loose
The knowledge of themselves.   *A drum a farre off.*

   Edg. Give me your hand far off me thinks I heare the beaten
Come father ile bestow you with a friend.   *Exit.*   (drum,

Enter Cordelia, Kent and Doctor.

                                       (thy goodnes,
   Cord. O thou good *Kent* how shall I live and worke to match
My life will be too short and every measure faile me.
   Kent. To be acknowledged madame is ore payd,
All my reports go with the modest truth,
Nor more, nor clipt, but so.
   Cor. Be better suited these weeds are memories of those
Worser howers, I prithe put them off.
   Kent. Pardon me deere madame,
Yet to be knowne shortens my made intent,
My boone I make it that you know me not,
Till time and I thinke meete.
   Cord. Then beet so, my good Lord how does the king.
   Doct. Madame sleepes still.   (nature,
   Cord. O you kind Gods cure this great breach in his abused
The untund and hurrying sences, O wind up
Of this child changed father.
   Doct. So please your Majestie that we may wake the king,
He hath slept long.
   Cord. Be governd by your knowledge and proceed,
Ith sway of your owne will is he arayd,
   Doct. I madam, in the heavinesse of his sleepe,
We put fresh garments on him,
   Gent. Good madam be by, when we do awake him
I doubt not of his temperance.
   Cord. Very well.
   Doct. Please you draw neere, louder the musicke there,
   Cor. O my deer father restoration hang thy medicin on my lips,
And let this kis repaire those violent harmes that my two sisters
Have in thy reverence made.

Kent. Kind and deere Princesse,

Cord. Had you not bene their father these white flakes,
Had challengd pitie of them, was this a face
To be exposd against the warring winds,
To stand against the deepe dread bolted thunder,
In the most terrible and nimble stroke
Of quick crosse lightning to watch poore *Per du,*
With this thin helme mine injurious dogge,
Though he had bit me, shoud have stood that night
Against my fire, and wast thou saine poore father,
To hovill thee with swine and rogues forlorne,
In short and mustie straw, alack, alack,
Tis wonder that thy life and wits at once
Had not concluded all, he wakes speake to him.

Doct. Madam do you, tis fittest.

Cord. How does my royall Lord, how fares your majestie.

Lear. You do me wrong to take me out ath grave,
Thou art a soule in blisse, but I am bound
Upon a wheele of fire, that mine owne teares
Do scald like molten lead.

Cord. Sir know me.

Lear. Yar a spirit I know, where did you dye.

Cord. Still, still, farre wide.

Doct. Hees scarce awake, let him alone a while.

Lear. Where have I bene, where am I faire day light,
I am mightily abusd, I should ene dye with pitie,
To see another thus, I know not what to say,
I will not sweare these are my hands, lets see,
I feele this pin pricke, would I were assur'd of my condition.

Cord. O looke upon me sir, and hold your hands in
benediction or'e me, no sir you must not kneele.

Lear. Pray doe not mocke,
I am a very foolish fond old man,
Fourescore and upward, and to deale plainly
I feare I am not in my perfect mind,
Mee thinks I should know you, and know this man;
Yet I am doubtfull, for I am mainly ignorant

What place this is, and all the skill I have
Remembers not these garments, nor I know not
Where I did lodge last night, doe not laugh at me,
For as I am a man, I thinke this Ladie
To be my child *Cordelia*.   *Cord.* And so I am.

 Lear. Be your teares wet, yes faith, I pray weep not,
If you have poyson for mee I will drinke it,
I know you doe not love me, for your sisters
Have as I doe remember, done me wrong,
You have some cause, they have not.

 Cord. No cause, no cause.   *Lear.* Am I in *France*?

 Kent. In your owne kingdome sir.

 Lear. Doe not abuse me?

 Doct. Be comforted good Madame, the great rage you see is cured in him, and yet it is danger to make him even ore the time hee hast lost, desire him to goe in, trouble him no more till further setling: *Cord.* Wilt please your highnes walke?

 Lear. You must beare with me, pray now forget and forgive,
I am old and foolish.   *Exeunt. Manet Kent and Gent.*

 Gent. Holds it true sir that the Duke of *Cornwall* was so slaine?

 Kent. Most certaine sir.

 Gent. Who is conductor of his people?

 Kent. As tis said, the bastard sonne of *Gloster*.

 Gent. They say *Edgar* his banisht sonne is with the Earle of *Kent* in *Germanie*.

 Kent. Report is changeable, tis time to looke about,
The powers of the kingdome approach apace.

 Gent. The arbiterment is like to be bloudie, fare you well sir.

 Kent. My poynt and period will be throughly wrought,
Or well, or ill, as this dayes battels fought.   *Exit.*

   Enter Edmund, Regan, and their powers.

 Bast. Know of the Duke if his last purpose hold,
Or whether since he is advis'd by ought
To change the course, hee's full of alteration
And selfe reproving, bring his constant pleasure.

[143]

Reg. Our sisters man is certainly miscaried.

Bast. Tis to be doubted Madam.

Reg. Now sweet Lord,
You know the goodnes I intend upon you,
Tell me but truly, but then speake the truth,
Doe you not love my sister?   *Bast.* I, honor'd love.

Reg. But have you never found my brothers way,
To the forfended place?   *Bast.* That thought abuses you.

Reg. I am doubtfull that you have beene conjunct and
bosom'd with hir, as far as we call hirs.

Bast. No by mine honour Madam.   (wih her.

Reg. I never shall indure hir, deere my Lord bee not familiar

Bast. Feare me not, shee and the Duke her husband.

Enter Albany and Gonorill with troupes.

Gono. I had rather loose the battaile, then that sister
should loosen him and mee.

Alb. Our very loving sister well be-met
For this I heare the King is come to his daughter
With others, whome the rigour of our state
Forst to crie out, where I could not be honest
I never yet was valiant, for this busines
It touches us, as *France* invades our land
Not bolds the King, with others whome I feare,
Most just and heavy causes make oppose.

Bast. Sir you speake nobly.   *Reg.* Why is this reason'd?

Gono. Combine togither gainst the enemy,
For these domestique dore particulars
Are not to question here.

Alb. Let us then determine with auntient of warre on our
proceedings. *Bast.* I shall attend you presently at your tent.

Reg. Sister you'l goe with us?   *Gon.* No.

Reg. Tis most convenient, pray you goe with us.

Gon. O ho, I know the riddle, I will goe.   *Enter Edgar*

Edg. If ere your Grace had speech with man so poore,
Heare me one word.   *Exeunt.*

Alb. Ile overtake you, speake.

Edg. Before you fight the battell ope this letter,
If you have victory let the trumpet sound
For him that brought it, wretched though I seeme,
I can produce a champion that will prove
What is avowched there, if you miscary,
Your busines of the world hath so an end,
Fortune love you,   *Alb.* Stay till I have read the letter.
    Edg. I was forbid it, when time shall serve let but the
Herald cry and ile appeare againe.   *Exit.*
    Alb. Why fare thee well, I will ore-looke the paper.

Enter Edmund.

Bast. The enemies in vew, draw up your powers
Hard is the quesse of their great strength and forces
By diligent discovery, but your hast is now urg'd on you.
    Alb. Wee will greet the time.   *Exit.*
    Bast. To both these sister have I sworne my love,
Each jealous of the other as the the sting are of the Adder,
Which of them shall I take, both one or neither, neither can bee
If both remaine alive, to take the widdow   (injoy'd
Exasperates, makes mad her sister *Gonorill,*
And hardly shall I cary out my side
Her husband being alive, now then we'le use
His countenadce for the battaile, which being done
Let her that would be rid of him devise
His speedie taking off, as for his mercy
Which he entends to *Lear* and to *Cordelia*:
The battaile done, and they within our power
Shall never see his pardon, for my state
Stands on me to defend, not to debate.   *Exit.*

*Alarum. Enter the powers of France over the stage, Cordelia with
her father in her hand.
Enter Edgar and Gloster.*

    Edg. Here father, take the shaddow of this bush
For your good hoast, pray that the right may thrive
If ever I returne to you againe ile bring you comfort. *Exit.*

[145]

Glost. Grace goe with you sir.   *Alarum and retreat.*

Edg. Away old man, give me thy hand, away,
King *Lear* hath lost, he and his daughter taine,
Give me thy hand, come on.

Glost. No farther sir, a man may rot even here.

Edg. What in ill thoughts againe men must indure,
Their going hence, even as their coming hither,
Ripenes is all come on.

Enter Edmund, with Lear and Cordelia prisoners.

Bast, Some officers take them away, good guard
Untill their greater pleasures best be knowne
That are to censure them.   (incurd

Cor. We are not the first who with best meaning have
The worst, for thee oppressed King am I cast downe,
My selfe could else outfrowne false Fortunes frowne,
Shall we not see these daughters, and these sisters?

Lear. No, no, come lets away to prison
We two alone will sing like birds it'h cage,
When thou dost aske me blessing, ile kneele downe
And aske of thee forgivenes, so weele live
And pray, and sing, and tell old tales and laugh
At guilded butterflies, and heare poore rogues
Talke of Court newes, and weele talke with them to,
Who looses, and who wins, whose in, whose out,
And take upon's the mistery of things
As if we were Gods spies, and weele weare out
In a wal'd prison, packs and sects of great ones
That ebbe and flow bith'Moone.

Bast. Take them away.

Lear. Upon such sacrifices my *Cordelia,*
The Gods themselves throw incense, have I caught thee?
He that parts us shall bring a brand from heaven,
And fire us hence like Foxes, wipe thine eyes,
The good shall devoure em, fleach and fell
Ere they shall make us weepe? wele see um starve first,

Bast. Come hither Captaine, harke.   (come.

Take thou this note, goe follow them to prison,
One step, I have advanct thee, if thou dost
As this instructs thee, thou dost make thy way
To noble fortunes, know thou this that men
Are as the time is, to be tender minded
Does not become a sword, thy great imployment
Will not beare question, either say thout do't,
Or thrive by other meanes.

    Cap. Ile do't my Lord.

    Bast. About it, and write happy when thou hast don,
Marke I say instantly, and carie it so
As I have set it downe.

    Cap. I cannot draw a cart, nor eate dride oats,
If it bee mans worke ile do't.

Enter Duke, the two Ladies, and others.

    Alb. Sir you have shewed to day your valiant strain,
And Fortune led you well, you have the captives
That were the opposites of this dayes strife,
We doe require then of you, so to use them,
As we shall find their merits, and our safty
May equally determine.

    Bast. Sir I thought it fit,
To send the old and miserable King to some retention, and ap-
Whose age has charmes in it whose title more, (pointed guard,
To pluck the common bossome of his side,
And turne our imprest launces in our eyes
Which doe commaund them, with him I sent the queen
My reason, all the same and they are readie to morrow,
Or at further space, to appeare where you shall hold
Your session at this time, wee sweat and bleed,
The friend hath lost his friend and the best quarrels
In the heat are curst, by those that feele their sharpnes,
The question of *Cordelia* and her father
Requires a fitter place.

    Alb. Sir by your patience,
I hold you but a subject of this warre, not as a brother.

[147]

Reg. That's as we lift to grace him,
Me thinkes our pleasure should have beene demanded
Ere you had spoke so farre, he led our powers,
Bore the commission of my place and person,
The which imediate may well stand up,
And call it selfe your brother.

Gono. Not so hot, in his owne grace hee doth exalt
himselfe more then in your advancement.

Reg. In my right by me invested he com-peers the best.

Gon. That were the most, if hee should husband you.

Reg. Jesters doe oft prove Prophets.

Gon. Hola, hola, that eye that told you so, lookt but a squint.

Reg. Lady I am not well, els I should answere
From a full flowing stomack, Generall
Take thou my souldiers, prisoners, patrimonie,
Witnes the world that I create thee here
My Lord and maister.

Gon. Meane you to injoy him then?

Alb. The let alone lies not in your good will.

Bast. Nor in thine Lord.

Alb. Halfe blouded fellow, yes.

Bast. Let the drum strike, and prove my title good.

Alb. Stay yet, heare reason, *Edmund* I arrest thee
On capitall treason, and in thine attaint,
This gilded Serpent, for your claime faire sister
I bare it in the interest of my wife,
Tis she is subcontracted to this Lord
And I her husband contradict the banes,
If you will mary, make your love to me,
My Lady is bespoke, thou art arm'd *Gloster*,
If none appeare to prove upon thy head,
Thy hainous, manifest, and many treasons,
There is my pledge, ile prove it on thy heart
Ere I tast bread, thou art in nothing lesse
Then I have here proclaimed thee.

Reg. Sicke, ô sicke.

Gon. If not, ile ne're trust poyson.

[148]

Bast. Ther's my exchange, what in the world he is,
That names me traytor, villain-like he lies,
Call by thy trumpet, he that dares approach,
On him, on you, who not, I will maintaine
My truth and honour firmely.
 Alb. A Herald ho. *Bast.* A Herald ho, a Herald.
 Alb. Trust to thy single vertue, for thy souldiers
All levied in my name, have in my name tooke their
 Reg. This sicknes growes upon me. (discharge.
 Alb. She is not well, convey her to my tent,
Come hether Herald, let the trumpet sound,
And read out this.   *Cap.* Sound trumpet?
 Her. If any man of qualitie or degree, in the hoast of the
army, will maintaine upon *Edmund* supposed Earle of *Gloster*,
that he's a manifold traitour, let him appeare at the third
sound of the trumpet, he is bold in his defence.
 Bast. Sound?   Againe?

  Enter Edgar at the third sound, a trumpet before him.

 Alb. Aske him his purposes why he appeares
Upon this call oth'trumpet.
 Her. What are you? your name and qualitie?
And why you answere this present summons.
 Edg. O know my name is lost by treasons tooth.
Bare-gnawne and canker-bitte; yet are I mov't
Where is the adversarie I come to cope with all.
 Alb. Which is that adversarie?   (*Gloster,*
 Edg. What's he that speakes for *Edmund* Earle of
 Bast. Him selfe, what saiest thou to him?
 Edg. Draw thy sword.
That if my speech offend a noble hart, thy arme
May do thee Justice, here is mine.
Behold it is the priviledge of my tongue,
My oath and my profession, I protest,
Maugure thy strength, youth, place and eminence,
Despight thy victor, sword and fire new fortun'd,
Thy valor and thy heart thou art a traytor.

[149]

False to thy Gods thy brother and thy Father,
Conspicuate gainst this high illustrious prince,
And from the'xtreamest upward of thy head,
To the descent and dust beneath thy feet,
A most toad-spotted traytor say thou no
This sword, this arme, and my best spirits,
As bent to prove upon thy heart whereto I speake thou liest,
   Bast. In wisdome I should aske thy name,
But since thy outside lookes so faire and warlike,
And that thy being some say of breeding breathes,
By right of knighthood, I disdaine and spurne
Heere do I tosse those treasons to thy head.
With the hell hatedly, oreturnd thy heart,
Which for they yet glance by and scarcely bruse,
This sword of mine shall give them instant way
Where they shall rest for ever, trumpets speake.
   Alb. Save him, save him.
   Gon. This is meere practise *Gloster* by the law of armes
Thou art not bound to answere an unknowne opposite,
Thou art not vanquisht, but cousned and beguild,
   Alb. Stop your mouth dame, or with this paper shall I
stople it, thou worse then any thing, reade thine owne evill,
nay no tearing Lady, I perceive you know't.   (me for't.
   Gon. Say if I do, the lawes are mine not thine, who shal arraine
   Alb. Most monstrous know'st thou this paper?
   Gon. Aske me not what I know.   *Exit. Gonorill.*
   Alb. Go after her, shee's desperate, governe her.
   Bast. What you have chargd me with, that have I don
And more, much more, the time will bring it out.
Tis past, and so am I, but what art thou
That hast this fortune on me? if thou bee'st noble
I do forgive thee.
   Edg. Let's exchange charity,
I am no lesse in bloud then thou art *Edmond*,
If more, the more thou hast wrongd me.
My name is *Edgar*, and thy fathers sonne,
The Gods are just, and of our pleasant vertues,

Make instruments to scourge us the darke and vitious
Place where thee he gotte, cost him his eies.

    Bast. Thou hast spoken truth, the wheele is come full
circled I am heere.

    Alb. Me thought thy very gate did prophecie,
A royall noblenesse I must embrace thee.
Let sorow split my heart if I did ever hate thee or thy father.

    Edg. Worthy Prince I know't.

    Alb. Where have you hid your selfe?
How have you knowne the miseries of your father?

    Edg. By nursing them my Lord,
List a briefe tale, and when tis told
O that my heart would burst the bloudy proclamation
To escape that followed me so neere,
O our lives sweetnes, that with the paine of death,
Would hourly die, rather then die at once.
Taught me to shift into mad-mans rags
To assume a semblance that very dogges disdain'd
And in this habit met I my father with his bleeding rings,
The precious stones new lost became his guide,
Led him, beg'd for him, sav'd him from dispaire,
Never (O Father) reveald my selfe unto him,
Untill some halfe houre past, when I was armed,
Not sure, though hoping of this good successe,
I askt his blessing, and from first to last,
Told him my pilgrimage, but his flawd heart,
Alacke too weake, the conflict to support,
Twixt two extreames of passion, joy and griefe,
Burst smillingly.

    Bast. This speech of yours hath moved me,
And shall perchance do good, but speake you on,
You looke as you had something more to say,

    Alb. If there be more, more wofull, hold it in,
For I am almost ready to dissolve, hearing of this,

    Edg. This would have seemed a periode to such
As love not sorow, but another to amplifie too much,
Would make much more, and top extreamitie

Whil'st I was big in clamor, came there in a man,
Who having seene me in my worst estate,
Shund my abhord society, but then finding
Who twas that so indur'd with his strong armes
He fastened on my necke and bellowed out,
As hee'd burst heaven, threw me on my father,
Told the most pitious tale of *Lear* and him,
That ever eare received, which in recounting
His griefe grew puissant and the strings of life,
Began to cracke twice then the trumpets sounded.
And there I left him traunst.
 Alb. But who was this.
 Ed. Kent sir, the banisht *Kent,* who in diguise,
Followed his enemie king and did him service
Improper for a slave.

    Enter one with a bloudie knife.

 Gent. Helpe, helpe,   (knife?
 Alb. What kind of helpe, what meanes that bloudy
 Gent. Its hot it smokes, it came even from the heart of –
 Alb. Who man, speake?
 Gent. Your Lady sir, your Lady, and her sister
By her is poysoned, she hath confest it.
 Bast. I was contracted to them both, all three
Now marie in an instant.
 Alb. Produce their bodies, be they alive or dead,
This Justice of the heavens that makes us tremble,
Touches us not with pity.   *Edg.* Here comes *Kent* sir.
 Alb. O tis he, the time will not allow   *Enter Kent*
The complement that very manners urges.
 Kent. I am come to bid my King and maister ay good night,
Is he not here?
 Duke. Great thing of us forgot,
Speake *Edmund,* whers the king, and whers *Cordelia*
Seest thou this object *Kent.*   *The bodies of Gonorill and*
 Kent. Alack why thus.   *Regan are brought in.*
 Bast. Yet *Edmund* was beloved,

      [152]

The one the other poysoned for my sake,
And after slue her selfe.   *Duke.* Even so, cover their faces.
   Bast. I pant for life, some good I meane to do,
Despight of my owne nature, quickly send,
Be briefe, int toth' castle for my writ,
Is on the life of *Lear* and on *Cordelia*,
Nay send in time.   *Duke.* Runne, runne, O runne.
   Edg. To who my Lord, who hath the office, send
Thy token of repreeve.
   Bast. Well thought on, take my sword the Captaine,
Give it the Captaine?   *Duke.* Hast thee for thy life.
   Bast. He hath Commission from thy wife and me,
To hang *Cordelia* in the prison, and to lay
The blame upon her owne despaire,
That she fordid her selfe.
   Duke. The Gods defend her, beare him hence a while.

Enter Lear with Cordelia in his armes.

   Lear. Howle, howle, howle, howle, O you are men of stones,
Had I your tongues and eyes, I would use them so,
That heavens vault should cracke, shees gone for ever,
I know when one is dead, and when one lives,
Shees dead as earth, lend me a looking glasse,
If that her breath will mist or staine the stone,
Why then she lives.   *Kent.* Is this the promist end.
   Edg. Or image of that horror.   *Duke.* Fall and cease.
   Lear. This feather stirs she lives, if it be so,
It is a chance which do's redeeme all sorowes
That ever I have felt.   *Kent.* A my good maister.
   Lear. Prethe away?   *Edg.* Tis noble *Kent* your friend.
   Lear. A plague upon your murderous traytors all,
I might have saved her, now shees gone for ever,
Cordelia, Cordelia, stay a little, ha,
What ist thou sayest, her voyce was ever soft,
Gentle and low, an excellent thing in women,
I kild the slave that was a hanging thee.
   Cap. Tis true my Lords, he did.

[153]

Lear. Did I not fellow? I have seene the day,
With my good biting Fauchon I would
Have made them skippe, I am old now,
And these same crosses spoyle me, who are you?
Mine eyes are not othe best, ile tell you straight.

   Kent. If Fortune bragd of two she loved or hated,
One of them we behold.   *Lear.* Are not you *Kent?*

   Kent. The same your servant *Kent*, where is your servant
Caius,

   Lear. Hees a good fellow, I can tell that,
Heele strike and quickly too, hees dead and rotten.

   Kent. No my good Lord, I am the very man.

   Lear. Ile see that straight.

   Kent. That from your life of difference and decay,
Have followed your sad steps.   *Lear.* You'r welcome hither.

   Kent. Nor no man else, als chearles, darke and deadly,
Your eldest daughters have foredoome themselves,
And desperatly are dead.   *Lear.* So thinke I to.

   Duke. He knowes not what he sees, and vaine it is,
That we present us to him.   *Edg.* Very bootlesse.   *Enter*
   Capt. Edmund is dead my Lord.   *Captaine.*

   Duke. Thats but a trifle heere, you Lords and noble friends,
Know our intent, what comfort to this decay may come,
shall be applied: for us we wil resigne during the life of this
old majesty, to him our absolute power, you to your rights
with boote, and such addition as your honor have more then
merited, all friends shall tast the wages of their vertue, and al
foes the cup of their deservings, O see, see.

   Lear. And my poore foole is hangd, no, no life, why should a
dog, a horse, a rat of life and thou no breath at all, O thou wilt
come no more, never, never, never, pray you undo this button,
thanke you sir, O,o,o,o.   *Edg.* He faints my Lord, my Lord.

   Lear. Breake hart, I prethe breake.   *Edgar.* Look up my Lord.

   Kent. Vex not his ghost, O let him passe,
He hates him that would upon the wracke,
Of this tough world stretch him out longer.

   Edg. O he is gone indeed.

Kent. The wonder is, he hath endured so long,
He but usurpt his life.

Duke. Beare them from hence, our present busines
Is to generall woe, friends of my soule, you twaine
Rule in this kingdome, and the goard state sustaine.

Kent. I have a journey sir, shortly to go,
My maister cals, and I must not say no.

Duke. The waight of this sad time we must obey,
Speake what we feele, not what we ought to say,
The oldest have borne most, we that are yong,
Shall never see so much, nor live so long.

FINIS.

Endnotes

Page 71

equalities: qualities.

moytie: share or portion.

Page 72

'tis our first intent: the Folio reading is 'fast', as in determined; but the Quarto's 'first', signifying principal, is equally acceptable as a reading. See Introduction, p. 27.

What shall Cordelia doe: later texts read 'What shall Cordelia speake'. The more active 'doe' is appropriate to Cordelia's greater vitality in the Quarto version.

Page 73

Then poore Cord: the abbreviated speech prefix for Cordelia has been used within the speech itself.

Page 74

The mistresse of Heccat and the might: i.e. the mysteries of Heccat and the might [of Heccat]. Hecate was the goddess of the lower world, and of magic.

Scythian: the barbarism of the Scythians was a conventional allusion.

Page 75

Vassall, recreant: the Folio prints this as 'O Vassall! Miscreant!' In the Folio text Lear uses 'recreant' shortly afterwards, addressing Kent ('Hear me, recreant! / On thine allegiance hear me') in its sense of one who proves false to his allegiance. In the Quarto the word is not present in this second speech. Its use in the first instance is clearly consistent with the intended meaning, and the Folio's substitution of 'Miscreant' an alternative reading rather than a necessary 'correction'.

Endnotes

Page 78
couldst: an alternative spelling of 'coldest'.

Not all the Dukes of watrish Burgundie: as well as an allusion to the well-watered landscape of Burgundy this is also possibly a criticism of the Duke's lack of spirit, cf. *Othello*, III, iii, 15.

benizon: blessing.

scanted: fallen short of, or undervalued.

Page 79
stand in the plague of custome: be subject to the conventional inhibitions placed on illegitimate sons.

mooneshines: months.

Page 80
Edmund the base shall tooth'legitimate: the eighteenth-century scholar, Thomas Edwards, suggested that 'too-' is a misreading of 'top' and that the line ought to read, 'Edmund the base shall top th'legitimate', i.e. overthrow Edgar, and possibly Gloster himself. The line can, however, be read in accordance with both Quarto and Folio, as an elliptical construction 'shall to the legitimate' – shall advance to, or take the place of, the legitimate.

an essay or tast of my vertue: 'tast' makes perfect sense as 'taste' – to sample, make trial of my virtue. Johnson suggested that 'essay' should read 'assay', 'tast' should read 'test', and that a metallurgical image was being used. The emendations produce a new meaning evidently not present in the original texts.

Page 81
aurigular: 'auricular' – by hearing.

Page 82
the Dragons taile . . . Ursa major: the Dragon's tale is an astrological term referring to the point of intersection of the orbit of the descending moon and the line of the Sun's orbit. Ursa major is the constellation of the Great Bear.

Page 83
sectary Astronomicall: a believer in astronomy.

Endnotes

Page 84
   obrayds: upbraids.

Page 85
   curious: complex or complicated.

Page 86
   clat-pole: clod-pate or blockhead.

Page 87
   lubbers: clumsy.

   gull: 'gall' – irritation or bitterness.

   hee must bee whipt out, when Ladie oth'e brach may stand by the fire and stink: brach in Shakespeare's day was generally used as a polite name for hound bitches. 'oth'e' is possibly a misreading that has been revised rather than corrected in the Folio.

Page 89
   frontlet: Lear appears to be referring to Gonorill's frowning forehead.

   Me thinks you are too much alate it'h frowne: 'too much of late i'the frown' – 'alate' presumably 'a'late' or 'o'late', contractions for the 'of late' that appears expanded in the Folio text.

Page 90
   deboyst: a variant of debauched.

   epicurisme: in its common sense of gluttony.

   kite: refers to the bird of prey.

   that it may live and be a thourt disvetur'd torment to her: 'thourt' and 'disvetur'd' seem to make no obvious sense. In this instance the Folio reading looks like an attempt to interpret an unintelligible reading.

Page 91
   with accent teares, fret channels in her cheeks: 'accent' is generally regarded as a compositorial error, misreading 'ardent' or 'aident' (meaning persistent or continual). Otherwise 'accent' used adjectivally to signify 'mark', together with 'fret', would have been recognised as the precise poetic descriptor that it clearly is.

Endnotes

y'are much more attaskt for want of wisedome: 'attaskt' presumably means something like 'taken to task', 'guilty of'. OED confidently defines the word as 'blame', though apparently on the basis of this context (or rather the same reading in the Folio) alone.

kibes: chilblains.

Not, I pray you what are they: it has been argued that the Quarto misplaces the punctuation mark which should follow 'I' and thus separate the Bastard's response to Curran's question, from his own question to Curran: 'Not I; pray you what are they?' But the Quarto's reading is still a possible variant, with 'not' used tersely as a negative reply.

lancht: lanced.

gasted: frightened.

make a dullard of the world: make the world appear stupid.

Lipsburie pinfold: enfolded or penned up between his lips, that is, in his teeth.

glassegazing: gazing into a mirror, i.e. vain.

cullyonly: a fool or a gull.

barber-munger: a fop who frequents barbers.

carbonado: cut, scotch or cross-hatch.

smoyle: 'smile' – presumably, as consistent with his disguise, Kent here slips into a rural accent.

Camulet: Camelot.

conjunct: in league with, or in support of, the king.

flechuent: this word appears as 'flechment' in the Folio: both readings thus seem derived from 'fleche', an arrow, possibly a coinage appropriate to the context. Modern editions turn Folio's 'flechment' into 'fleshment' (the action of 'fleshing'), an interpretation then established in the OED on the basis of this emendation.

Endnotes

Is such as basest and temnest wretches for pilferings / And most common trespasses are punisht with: uncorrected Quarto sheets show 'contaned' in place of 'temnest'. 'Temnest' is possibly therefore a contraction of 'contemnest', clarified by Capell's emendation to 'contemned'st'.

Page 102

president: precedent or example.

Bedlam beggars: Bedlam beggars were those who were able to avoid some of the restraints placed on beggars by parish officials, through being able to claim licences to beg on account of having spent time in the Bethlehem (Bedlam) asylum.

poor Turlygod: a number of possible explanations for 'Turlygod', a word not otherwise known, have been proposed. In the eighteenth century, Warburton suggested it was a corruption of 'Turlepin', the name of a band of naked beggars found in fourteenth-century Europe, with whom, like the Bedlam beggars, Edgar is linking himself.

Page 103

O how this mother swells up towards my hart / Historica passio: Lear alludes to a state of giddiness thought to particularly affect pregnant women, to begin in the womb and to swell toward the heart.

Page 107

Squire-like pension bag: 'bag', presumably 'beg'.

Page 108

imbossed: swollen, like the boss or raised centre of a shield.

depositaries: trustees.

Page 111

assurance: trustworthy information.

catericks: cataracts.

Hircanios: hurricanes.

Page 112

vaunt-currers: scouts or harbingers.

Page 113

caytife: wretch.

[160]

Endnotes

Ther's part of a power already landed: this creates a more immediate impression than the Folio's 'already footed'. See the 'Introduction' to this edition (page 38).

beates: pulsates there, i.e. filial ingratitude.

wore gloves in my cap: displayed his lady's favour.

hay no on ny, Dolphin my boy, my boy, caese let him trot by: 'on ny' is evidently part of a garbled song refrain. 'Dolphin' is used apparently as the name of a horse. 'Caese' could be 'cease', certainly simpler than Folio's 'sesey', which finds its way into modern editions through Malone's emendation 'sessa!'

sallets: salads.

whipt from tithing to tithing: vagabonds were moved on from parish to parish.

swithald footed: Swithald is presumably an allusion either to St Withold, mentioned in *The Troublesome Reign of King John* (1591) or, more plausibly, to St Swithin who was a popular early English saint associated with both rain and healing.

learned Theban: i.e. a Greek sage from the city of Thebes.

apprehension: arrest.

Justice: judge.

come ore the broome Bessy to mee: Capell, in his 1768 edition of the play, corrected 'broome' to 'Bourne', on the authority of what he identified as the popular song, printed around 1558 (see *Harleian Miscellany*, x, 260). 'Bourne' thus links with 'boat'. But it is also possible to cross over 'broom', and since broom grows on the banks of rivers, there is no pressing reason to emend.

Hoppedance cries in Toms belly: Hoppedance (Hoberdidance), along with Fratteretto and Fliberdigibet, all mentioned by Edgar, were devils.

[161]

Endnotes

yokefellow: partner.

joyne stoole: a low stool with three or four legs.

Page 122
festunate: urgent.

questrits: a Shakespearean coinage – 'questrists' – those on a quest or questing, set here as 'questrits'.

Page 123
Naughty: wicked.

Page 124
abus'd: wronged and deceived.

Page 125
dungell: dunghill.

Page 126
As flies are toth'wanton boyes, are we toth'Gods, / They bitt us for their sport: although both Quarto and Folio versions agree on the use of 'bitt' (bite), later versions arbitrarily amend this word to 'kill'. If gods are not normally thought of as 'biting', flies certainly are, and the notion of biting or tormenting is certainly appropriate to Gloster's sentiment here.

parrell: apparell, clothing.

Page 127
horse way: bridlepath.

Page 128
Whose reverance even the head-lugd bear would lick: 'head-lugd' means tugged or led by the head like, in this case, a bear in a halter.

Page 129
noyseles: unstirring, particularly without the noise of preparation for war.

Page 130
another way the newes is not so tooke: later editions correct 'tooke' to 'tart' as in sharp or grievous, but 'tooke' (taken, apprehended) also makes sense.

smilets: small smiles.

Endnotes

Page 131
    verball question: comment.

    conditions: character.

Page 132
    fermiter and furow weeds: rank and bitter herbs.

    beaydent and remediat: a typesetting error has lost the space between 'be' and 'aydent', that is, to be of aid, to be helpful.

Page 133
    Shee gave strange aliads, and most speaking lookes: 'aliads' has been variously interpreted, most inventively in Folios II–IV as 'Iliads'. 'Aliads' is presumably a simplified form of 'œilliads', defined as amorous glances.

Page 134
    sampire: an aromatic herb using in pickling.

    cock: a cock boat was a small ship's boat.

    boui: buoy.

Page 135
    opposles: irresistible.

    conceit: imagination, specifically a delusion.

    borne: boundary.

Page 136
    welkt: twisted.

    crow keeper: scarecrow.

    tricke: peculiarity.

Page 137
    forkes: legs.

    fichew: pole-cat.

    squiny: squint.

Page 138
    beadle: parish constable.

    a man of salt: a man of tears.

Endnotes

Page 139
Chill not let goe sir without cagion: this speech, and those of Edgar following, are transcribed in a rural dialect.

Page 140
your affectionate servant and for you her own for Venter, Gonorill: 'venter', 'venture': Gonorill's meaning is that she will belong to Edmund if he is prepared to 'venture on' the plot they have discussed.

ingenious: conscious.

Page 141
bestow: lodge.

Page 142
wide: astray, unfocused.

Page 143
rage: delirium.

arbiterment: decisive encounter.

Page 144
forfended: forbidden.

touches: concerns.

dore: a possible misprint for dear, or important.

with auntient of warre: with experienced officers.

Page 148
com-peers: equals.

Page 150
conspicuate: the Folio preferred 'conspirant' ('conspiring against'), but 'conspicuate' (conspicuous) is perfectly possible – 'conspicuate against', 'manifest in your opposition to' Albany.

toad-spotted: stained as the toad who was thought to be spotted with venom.

cousned and beguiled: cheated and deceived.

Page 154
Fauchon: a light sword.

Appendix

M. William Shak-speare

HIS
Historie, of King Lear.

Enter Kent, Gloster, and Bastard.

Kent.

I Thought the King had more affected the Duke of *Albany* then *Cornwell.*

Glost. It did allwaies seeme so to vs, but now in the diuision of the kingdomes, it appeares not which of the Dukes he values most, for equalities are so weighed, that curiositie in neither, can make choise of eithers moytie.

Kent. Is not this your sonne my Lord?

Glost. His breeding sir hath beene at my charge, I haue so often blusht to acknowledge him, that now I am braz'd to it.

Kent. I cannot conceiue you.

Glost. Sir, this young fellowes mother Could, wherupon shee grew round wombed. and had indeed Sir a sonne for her cradle, ere she had a husband for her bed, doe you smell a fault?

Kent. I cannot wish the fault vndone, the issue of it being so proper.

Glost. But I haue sir a sonne by order of Law, some yeare elder then this, who yet is no deerer in my account, though this knaue came something sawcely into the world before hee was sent for, yet was his mother faire, there was good sport at his makeing, & the whoreson must be acknowledged, do you know this noble gentleman *Edmund?*

B   *Bast.*

5

10

15

20

25

Bast. No my Lord.

Gloss. My Lord of Kent, remember him hereafter as my honorable friend.

Bast. My seruices to your Lordship.

30   *Kent.* I must loue you, and sue to know you better.

Bast. Sir I shall study deseruing.

Gloss. Hee hath beene out nine yeares, and away hee shall againe, the King is comming.

Sound a Sennet, Enter one bearing a Coronet, then Lear, then the Dukes of Albany, and Cornwell, next Gonorill, Regan, Cordelia, with followers.

35   *Lear.* Attend my Lords of France and Burgundy, *Gloster.*

Gloss. I shall my Leige.

Lear. Meane time we will expresse our darker purposes,
The map there; know we haue diuided
In three, our kingdome; and tis our first intent,
To shake all cares and busines of our state,

41   Confirming them on yonger yeares,

46   The two great Princes *France* and *Burgundy,*
Great ryuals in our youngest daughters loue,
Long in our Court haue made their amorous soiourne,

49   And here are to be answerd, tell me my daughters,

52   Which of you shall we say doth loue vs most,
That we our largest bountie may extend,
Where merit doth most challenge it,

55   *Gonorill* our eldest borne, speake first?

Gon. Sir I do loue you more then words can weild the
Dearer then eye-sight, space or libertie,   (matter,
Beyond what can be valued rich or rare,
No lesse then life; with grace, health, beautie, honour,

60   As much a child ere loued, or father friend,
A loue that makes breath poore, and speech vnable,
Beyond all manner of so much I loue you.

Cor. What shall *Cordelia* doe, loue and be silent.

Lear. Of al these bounds, euen from this line to this,

65   With shady forrests, and wide skirted meades,
We make thee Lady, to thine and *Albaines* issue,
Be this perpetuall, what saies our second daughter?

Our

Our deerest *Regan*, wife to *Cornwell*, speake?

    Reg. Sir I am made of the selfe same mettall that my sister is.   70
And prize me at her worth in my true heart.
I find she names my very deed of loue, onely she came short,   75
That I professe my selfe an enemie to all other ioyes,
Which the most precious square of sence possesses,
And find I am alone felicitate, in your deere highnes loue.

    Cord. Then poore *Cord.* & yet not so, since I am sure
My loues more richer then my tongue.   80

    Lear. To thee and thine hereditarie euer
Remaine this ample third of our faire kingdome,
No lesse in space, validity, and pleasure,
Then that confirm'd on *Gonorill*, but now our ioy,
Although the last, not least in our deere loue,   85
What can you say to win a third, more opulent   87
Then your sisters.

    Cord. Nothing my Lord.   (againe.   89

    Lear. How, nothing can come of nothing, speake   92

    Cord. Vnhappie that I am, I cannot heaue my heart into my
mouth, I loue your Maiestie according to my bond, nor more nor
lesse.   95

    Lear. Goe to, goe to, mend your speech a little,
Least it may mar your fortunes.

    Cord. Good my Lord,
You haue begot me, bred me, loued me,
I returne those duties backe as are right fit,
Obey you, loue you, and most honour you,   100
Why haue my sisters husbands if they say they loue you all,
Happely when I shall wed, that Lord whose hand
Must take my plight, shall cary halfe my loue with him,
Halfe my care and duty, sure I shall neuer
Mary like my sisters, to loue my father all.   105

    Lear. But goes this with thy heart ?

    Cord. I good my Lord.

    Lear. So yong and so vntender,

    Cord. So yong my Lord and true.

    Lear. Well let it be so, thy truth then be thy dower,   110
For by the sacred radience of the Sunne,

    B 2   The